knitsimple™

Clever tips & techniques
to guarantee success

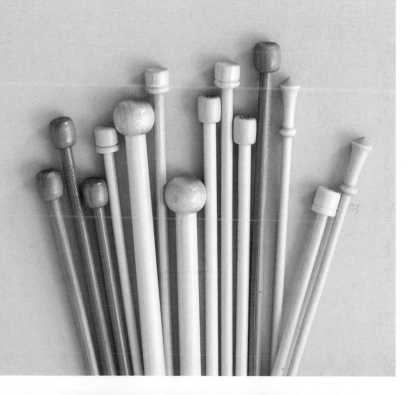

sixth&spring books
New York, New York

table of contents

99

95

61

61

71

83

137

65

87

Introduction

As we celebrate the first five years of *Knit Simple* magazine, I am thrilled to bring you this special collection of the most popular designs from our archives.

Knitting Workshops presents a full range of patterns, terms to know, must-have products and a list of essential reference books—all in one convenient spot. Included here are knits for women, men, children, babies and the home. We strive to present projects that are not only easy to make, but also stylish and timeless. All of these workshops highlight a specific technique, teach readers something new, and proceed step by step through the completion of a project.

From the most basic garments to the more complicated stitches and fashion projects, we cover many techniques that have helped take our readers' skills to the next level. *Knit Simple* readers love fashion accessories—warm hats, cozy scarves, socks and mittens. As a special feature, we have included charts for creating these accessories in a wide range of sizes, from infant to adult male and every family member in between.

And, finally, there's something for every skill level. Beginners can build knitting knowledge with projects ranging from a simple garter-stitch blanket to a stunning mosaic-stitch scarf. For those who already have the basics under their belts, there are plenty of challenges, like the A-line coat and the little girl's decked-out cardigan.

We hope *Knitting Workshops* will have a special place in your library for many years to come, and we are sure you will refer back to it many times as your knitting continues to grow.

Carla Scott, Editor-in-Chief, *Knit Simple* magazine

Cool Tools

Colorful, useful and oh-so-essential, the best in knitting accessories will keep you stitching in style.

a. Heart-shaped **Memoric Stitch Markers** by KA Classic Bamboo put a little love into every row. accessoriesunlimitedinc.com. **b.** Zip your knitting notions securely into a **Kritter Case** by Clover. clover-usa.com. **c.** Namaste's chic **Circular Case** keeps circular needles neatlyorganized, labeled and ready to pick up and go. namasteinc.com. **d.** The light, flexible **Carrie Soaking Tub** by Soak does double duty as a tote and wash bucket. soakwash.com. **e.** Brightly hued **Rollfix tape measures** are easy to spot across the room. purlsoho.com. **f.** Track your progress in the **Knit Witty project organizer**, with calculator, mechanical pencil and internal pockets. toknitorknot.com. **g.** Intoxicatingly scented **Soak Wash** treats fine fibers with care. soakwash.com. **h.** Hokey Croquis' **Fashionflat Sketchpad** features pro-quality drawing paper printed with body outlines that disappear when scanned or photocopied— a must for sketching out your own knitting designs. hokeycroquis.com.

Cool Tools

a. ChiaoGoo's aluminum **Tiny Tools Cases**—with pocket clips!—corral smaller-sized tools. chiaogoo.com. **b.** Kiku's whimsical **handmade needles** are too awesome to resist. kiku-co.com. **c.** Make short work of your skeins with The Woolery's **Tabletop Yarn Swift**. It sets up in moments—no clamp needed. woolery.com. **d.** Colonial Needle Company's exquisite **Rosewood Interchangeable Needle** set comes in a silk carrying case and includes myriad accessories. colonialneedle.com. **e.** Parkhaus **Poet's Cases**, made from felted lamb's wool, have a hip, creative vibe. parkhausberlin.de/collection/accessories. **f.** The compact, clever **Knit Kit** packs in scissors, stitch markers, point protectors, crochet hook, tape measure, thread cutter and more. theknitkit.com. **g.** KA Classic Bamboo's **Miniature Needle Set** is a must-have for small-scale projects. accessoriesunlimitedinc.com. **h.** No more guessing at yarn weight—EatSmart's **Precision Pro Multifunction Digital Kitchen Scale** measures in grams and ounces. eatsmartproducts.com. **i.** Namaste's supercute **Cali Collection Mini Clutch** has a retro kisslock closure and detachable shoulder strap. namasteinc.com.

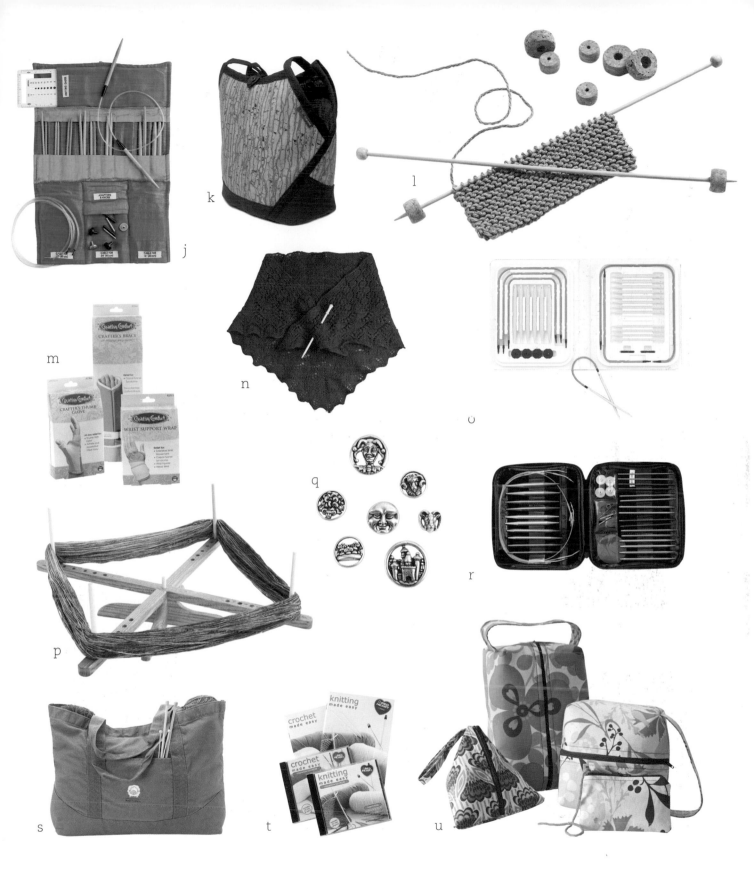

j. The versatile **Webs Interchangeable Needle Set** features bamboo needles and a plethora of tools. yarn.com. **k.** Tom Bihn's popular **Swift Bag** is now offered in a gorgeous cork fabric. tombihn.com. **l.** Colonial Needle's **StitchCorkers** come in four sizes to hold stitches securely. colonialneedle.com. **m. Creative Comfort** braces and wraps bring relief to aching joints. joann.com. **n.** Brittany's lovely **Shawl Pins** are workshop-crafted from birchwood. brittanyneedles.com. **o.** Denise **Interchangeable Knitting Needle Set** packs in all you need at the right price. knitdenise.com. **p.** ChiaoGoo's **Yarn Swift** is an ingenious tabletop tool of Amish design. chiaogoo.com. **q.** Pewter buttons in various styles from Nicky Epstein's **Royal Button Collection**. nickyknits.com. **r.** Aluminum-needle devotees will love Boye's color-coded **Needle Master Interchangeable Needle System**. simplicity.com. **s.** Knit Happy's canvas **Everything Tote** swallows even your biggest project. iknithappy.com. **t.** Brush up on the basics with Coats & Clark's **Learn How** CD and booklet series. coatsandclark.com. **u.** Just looking at RoseKnits' festive project totes will cheer you up. Pictured, left to right: **Fortune Cookie Tote**, **Box Totes** and **Notions Pouch**. etsy.com/shop/roseknits.

Ready for a good read? Try a new pattern, develop some new skills or just enjoy all the colorful eye candy in these exceptional books.

Your Knitting Library

60 Quick Knits,
by Tanis Gray
(Sixth&Spring Books;
$17.95) The incredibly
versatile Cascade
220 yarn stars in this
collection of sixty all-
new patterns for every
season. With twenty
designs each for hats,
scarves and mittens,
this book is a go-to
guide for knitting gifts
everyone will love.

The Stitch Collection,
by Debbie O'Neill
(Lark Books; $19.95)
Consider this a boxed
set of the knitter's hit
parade. Five volumes
of about sixty swatch-
filled pages each—
in the categories of
Knit & Purl, Rib, Lace,
Cables and Specialty—
are packaged in one
handy box for easy
shelving and toting.

Lily Chin's Knitting
Tips & Tricks, by Lily
Chin (Potter Craft;
$16.99) Get a leg
up in your favorite
craft with this title, a
printed version of
Chin's popular tips-
and-techniques
classes, which she's
taught to great ac-
claim at local yarn
shops nationwide for
more than a decade.

One-Skein Wonders,
by Judith Durant (Storey
Publishing; $18.95)
Organized by project type
and fiber weight, this pat-
tern-packed book helps
you stitch through your
stash in a flash. Turn left-
overs and impulse-buy
hanks into fabulous hats,
scarves, socks, bags and
countless other imagina-
tive creations using just
one ball of yarn.

The Big Book of Socks,
by Kathleen Taylor
(Taunton Press; $24.95)
The "Big" in the title is
not false advertising.
You'll find seventy-five
patterns here, enough
to keep even the
quickest stitcher busy
for some time. The first
chapter is devoted to
tube socks, the easiest
way to get your feet
wet, so to speak.

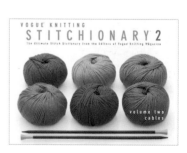

Vogue Knitting Stitchionary
Volume 1: Knit & Purl, by
the editors of *Vogue Knitting*
(Sixth&Spring Books; $29.95)
For this first volume in the
exceptional reference series,
Vogue Knitting magazine's
editors pored over twenty-
plus years of issues, compiling
basic and special stitch patterns and presenting them
in crystal-clear swatch photos
with charted and written
instructions.

Design It, Knit It,
by Debbie Bliss
(Sixth&Spring Books;
$24.95) Get a bird's-
eye view of a master
knitter at work as
Bliss demystifies her
design process. The
five main chapters—
which delve into shap-
ing, colorwork, texture,
kids' knits and details
—each include three
signature Bliss patterns.

Classic Knits,
by Erika Knight
(Potter Craft; $19.95)
Take high-quality
yarns, combine them
with Knight's clean,
confident aesthetic,
and voilà—beautifully
detailed basic sweaters
and garments for the
luxe life—V necks,
shrugs, camisoles and
other silky treats that
you'll treasure.

Vogue Knitting Stitchionary
Volume 2: Cables, by the
editors of *Vogue Knitting*
(Sixth&Spring Books; $29.95)
The second volume in *Vogue*
Knitting's acclaimed stitch dic-
tionary series is a stupendous
all-you-can-knit buffet of
exciting cables, from the sim-
plest to the most extraordinary.
Arranged in order of difficulty,
the swatches, instructions
and charts will give neophytes
the confidence to cable.

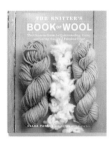

The Knitter's Book of Wool, by Clara Parkes (Potter Craft; $30) Nineteen lovely projects anchor this book, but before you get there, study up on the nearly ninety-page introduction to pasture-to-pattern thinking. You'll learn to consider sheep breeds and how quality differs from one wool fiber to the next.

Tips for Knitters, by Debbie Bliss (Trafalgar Square; $19.95) This spiral-bound primer from one of Britain's premier knitwear designers is full of stitchy advice. The eleven chapters brim with info on how to do everything from choosing the right buttons to distinguishing Aran yarn from chunky.

Vogue Knitting: The Ultimate Knitting Book, by the editors of Vogue Knitting (Sixth&Spring Books; $38.95) This essential text is the most comprehensive book on knitting that you'll find. With input from more than fifty industry leaders plus exhaustive coverage of techniques for all levels of skill, it's a must-have reference for a knitter's library. Included are tool guides and a history of the craft.

Knitting in Plain English, by Maggie Righetti (St. Martin's Press; $17.95) In this revised edition of her classic, originally published in 1986, the outspoken Righetti tells it like it is when it comes to perfecting your knitting. This essential beginner's text is more than helpful— it's fun reading, too.

Finishing Techniques for Hand Knitters, by Sharon Brant (Trafalgar Square; $24.95) Without proper finishing, even the best-knit pieces form a shoddy garment. Brant comes to the rescue with a guide chock-full of detailed how-tos and some handsome practice patterns at the end.

Knitting a Kiss in Every Stitch, by Nicky Epstein (Sixth&Spring Books; $19.95) Here's a pretty package for knitters who like gift stitching almost as much as, if not more than, making things for themselves. Thirty-six patterns from master knitter Epstein are here (the majority of them rated "easy"), as well as three pages listing charities you can knit for once you've finished with your entire gift list.

Knitalong, by Larissa and Martin John Brown (STC; $22.50) Celebrating the joy of knitting as a social event, this books of photos and essays reveals a fascinating world. From online crazes to fundraising drives to Stitch 'N Pitch ballgames, all kinds of group-knitting happenings are covered. Also presented are a few patterns (a bias-knit afghan, an iconic "Meathead" hat).

Knitted Toys, by Zoë Mellor (North Light Books; $19.99) A bright, old-fashioned knitted critter stands out among all the plastic and noisy technology found in modern-day toy chests. These twenty-five cheerful pals (including a gingerbread man and a patchwork turtle) are easy to knit and love.

Never Too Old to Knit, by Karin Strom (Sixth&Spring Books; $24.95) This is your grandma's knitting! But make no mistake, this book is for a modern, hip breed of grandma who might not be an expert knitter and needs a guide that addresses her issues and sensibilities. Elegant garments, charity knitting and baby items are on the agenda here, as is getting out and bonding with like-minded peers.

Easy and logical, these standard abbreviations are the shorthand of knitting and crochet.

Terms to Know

hand-knitting abbreviations

approx approximately
beg begin(ning)
CC contrasting color
cm centimeter(s)
cn cable needle
cont continue(ing)
dec decrease(ing)
dpn double pointed needle(s)
foll follow(s)(ing)
g gram(s)
grp(s) group(s)
inc increase(ing)
k knit
K2tog Knit 2 stitches together— 1 stitch decreased
kfb knit into front and back of a stitch
LH left-hand
m meter(s)
mm millimeter(s)
MC main color
M1 make one (see glossary)
M1 p-st make 1 purl stitch

oz ounce(s)
p purl
P2tog purl 2 stitches together— 1 stitch decreased
pat(s) pattern(s)
pm place marker
psso pass slip stitch(es) over
rem remain(s)(ing)
rep repeat
rev St st reverse-stockinette stitch
RH right-hand
RS right side
rnd(s) round(s)
SKP slip 1, knit 1, pass slip stitch(es) over—1 stitch decreased
SK2P slip 1, knit 2 stitches together, pass slip stitch(es) over— 2 stitches decreased
S2KP slip 2 stitches together knitwise, knit 1, pass slip stitches over knit 1—2 stitches

decreased
sl slip
sl st slip stitch (U.K.: see glossary)
ssk slip, slip, knit (see glossary)
ssp slip, slip, purl (see glossary)
st(s) stitch(es)
St st stockinette stitch (U.K.: see basic stitches)
tbl through back loop(s)
tog together
WS wrong side(s)
wyib with yarn in back
wyif with yarn in front
yd yard(s)
yo yarn over (hook or needle) (U.K.: see glossary)
* repeat directions following * as many times as indicated
[ ] repeat directions inside brackets as many times as indicated

crochet abbreviations

BP back post
BPdc back post double crochet
BPsc back post single crochet
BPtr back post treble crochet
ch chain(s)
ch- refers to chain or space previously made (i.e., ch-1 space)
ch-sp chain space previously made
dc double crochet (U.K.: tr—treble)
dc2tog double crochet 2 stitches together

dtr double treble (U.K.: trtr—triple treble)
FP front post
FPdc front post double crochet
FPsc front post single crochet
FPtr front post treble crochet
grp(s) group(s)
hdc half double crochet (U.K.: htr—half treble)
lp(s) loop(s)
sc single crochet (U.K.: dc —double crochet)

sc2tog single crochet 2 sts together
sk skip(ped)
sl st slip stitch (U.K.: sc—single crochet)
sp(s) space(s)
t-ch turning chain
tr treble (U.K.: dtr—double treble)
trtr triple treble (U.K.: qtr—quadruple treble)

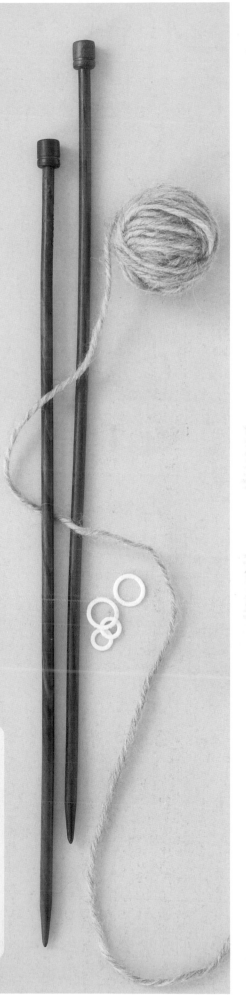

crochet **hooks**

U.S.	Metric
B/1	2.25mm
C/2	2.75mm
D/3	3.25mm
E/4	3.5mm
F/5	3.75mm
G/6	4mm
7	4.5mm
H/8	5mm
I/9	5.5mm
J/10	6mm
K/10½	6.5mm
L/11	8mm
M/13	9mm
N/15	10mm

knitting **needles**

U.S.	Metric
0	2mm
1	2.25mm
2	2.75mm
3	3.25mm
4	3.5mm
5	3.75mm
6	4mm
7	4.5mm
8	5mm
9	5.5mm
10	6mm
10½	6.5mm
11	8mm
13	9mm
15	10mm
17	12.75mm
19	15mm
35	19mm

skill levels
for knitting & crochet

1 Beginner
Ideal first project.

2 Easy
Basic stitches, minimal shaping, simple finishing.

3 Intermediate
For knitters/crocheters with some experience. More intricate stitches, shaping and finishing.

4 Experienced
For knitters/crocheters able to work patterns with complicated shaping and finishing.

measuring

To measure your knitting, lay the fabric out on a flat, smooth surface and take the measurement in the middle of a row using a tape measure. Don't measure an armhole along the curve or slanted edges.

blocking

Block or press garment pieces according to the instructions included in the pattern and on the yarn label. The best method of blocking is to pin the knit pieces to a padded surface, lightly dampen them and remove when dry.

Glossary

BIND OFF

To finish off an edge and keep stitches from unraveling by lifting the first stitch over the second, the second over the third, etc. (U.K.: cast off)

BIND OFF IN RIBBING

Maintain the rib pattern as you bind off (knit the knit stitches; purl the purl stitches). (U.K.: cast off in ribbing)

CAST ON

Form a foundation row by making a specified number of loops on the knitting needle.

DECREASE

Reduce the number of stitches in a row (i.e., knit 2 together; purl 2 together).

INCREASE

Add to the number of stitches in a row (i.e., knit in front and back of stitch).

KNITWISE

Insert the needle into the stitch as if you were going to knit it.

MAKE ONE

With tip of needle, lift strand between last stitch knit and next stitch on left-hand needle, place strand on left-hand needle and knit into back of it to increase one stitch.

PLACE MARKERS

Loop a piece of contrasting yarn or a purchased stitch marker onto the needle.

PICK UP AND KNIT (PURL)

Knit (or purl) into the loops along an edge.

PURLWISE

Insert the needle into the stitch as if you were going to purl it.

SELVAGE STITCH

Edge stitch that helps make seaming easier.

SKIP

Skip specified number of stitches of the previous row and work into next stitch. (U.K.: miss)

SLIP, SLIP, KNIT (PURL)

Slip next two sts knitwise (purlwise), one at a time, to right-hand needle. Insert tip of left-hand needle into fronts of these sts from left to right and knit (purl) them together to decrease one st.

SLIP STITCH

In knitting, pass a stitch from the left-hand to the right-hand needle as if to purl without working it. **In crochet,** insert hook through loop or edge, yarn over and pull through loop on hook. (U.K.: abbreviation—ss or sc)

WORK EVEN

Continue in specified pattern without increasing or decreasing. (U.K.: work straight)

YARN OVER

In knitting, make a new stitch by placing the yarn over the right-hand needle. (U.K.: yfwd, yon, yrn) **In crochet,** wind yarn around hook. (U.K.: yoh or yrh)

about sizing

Pattern instructions are given for the smallest size, with the larger sizes in parentheses. If only one figure is given, it applies to all sizes.

choosing size

To decide which size to make, measure a favorite sweater to use as a guide. Choose the finished bust/chest measurement in the pattern that comes closest to your desired width.

the gauge

Knitting gauge—the number of stitches and rows per inch—determines the size of the garment you are making. Every knitting pattern states the gauge, or "tension," on which the sizing is based. For successful results, it is essential to test your knitting against this measurement before you start a project. Make a test swatch at least 4"/10cm square, using the yarn and needle size called for in the pattern. Then measure your swatch using a ruler or a knit gauge tool, pictured at right. If the number of stitches and rows does not match the pattern's gauge, you must change your needle size. An easy rule to follow is: TO GET FEWER STITCHES TO THE INCH/CM, USE A LARGER NEEDLE; TO GET MORE STITCHES TO THE INCH/CM, USE A SMALLER NEEDLE. Try different needle sizes until you get the proper gauge.

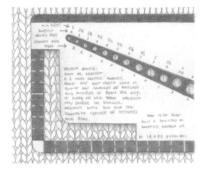

basic stitches

Garter stitch
Knit every row. For circular knitting: Knit one round, then purl one round.

Stockinette stitch
Knit right-side rows and purl wrong-side rows. For circular knitting: Knit all rounds.
(U.K.: stocking stitch)

Reverse-stockinette stitch
Purl right-side rows and knit wrong-side rows. For circular knitting: Purl all rounds.
(U.K.: reverse stocking stitch)

K1, P1 ribbing
Row 1: *K1, p1; rep from *.
Row 2: K the knit sts and p the purl sts. Rep row 2 for k1, p1 rib.

reading instructions

Before starting to knit, read through the entire set of instructions. Circle the information for your size and look up unfamiliar terms. Study the schematics for measurements and shapes of the pieces and determine if you want to make any changes. If you make alterations, be sure to adjust the yarn amounts accordingly.

substituting yarns

Using the yarn specified in each pattern will give you the best results. If you need to substitute a yarn, compare the new yarn with the yarn strands shown with each pattern. Make a gauge swatch with the substitute yarn to be sure that it matches the original gauge and has a similar appearance.

binding off

This process finishes off the edges of a garment to prevent them from unraveling. The most popular bind-off method for finishing knitting is: Knit two stitches. *Insert the point of the left-hand needle (LHN) into the first stitch on the right-hand needle (RHN). With the point of the LHN, pull this stitch over the second stitch on the RHN and off the needle. You have completed one bind-off, and one stitch remains on the RHN. Knit the next stitch. Repeat from * until you have bound off the required number of stitches. When one stitch remains on the RHN, pull the yarn end through the loop to fasten off.

frequently asked questions

What size should I make?
Measure a favorite sweater to use as a guide, and choose a size by the finished bust/chest measurements in the pattern.

Which yarn should I use?
The yarn we have specified will give you the best results. Compare substitutions to the yarn strands shown on the yarn photos that accompany each pattern.

Can I change needle or hook sizes?
Each pattern suggests a size and says OR SIZE TO OBTAIN GAUGE. See the gauge explanation above, and use any size that will give you the correct gauge.

How can I find out more?
Bookstores and libraries carry a vast array of comprehensive learn-to-knit books; or visit **www.learntoknit.com**.

Tools of the Trade

These tools and accessories bring accuracy and ease to your favorite hobby.

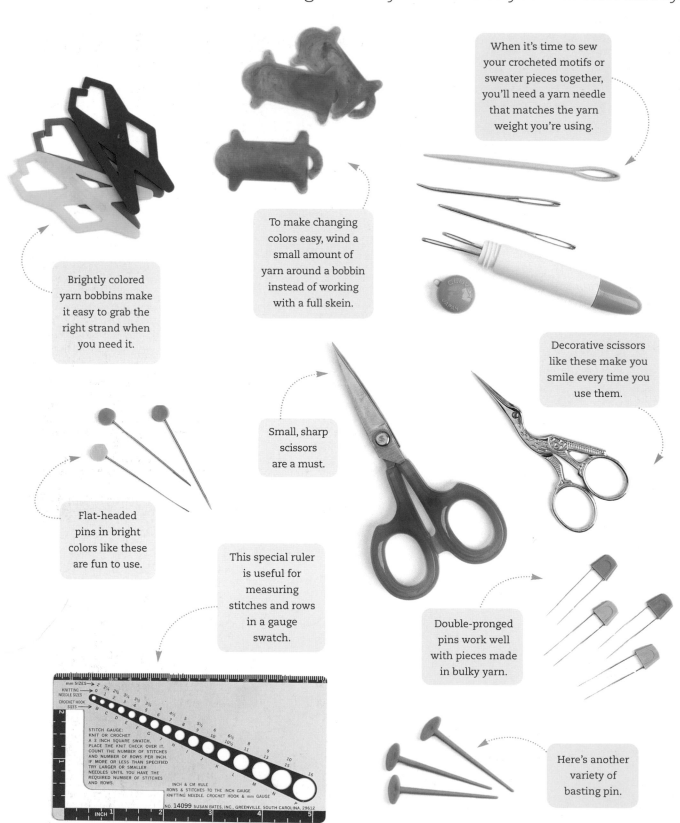

When it's time to sew your crocheted motifs or sweater pieces together, you'll need a yarn needle that matches the yarn weight you're using.

To make changing colors easy, wind a small amount of yarn around a bobbin instead of working with a full skein.

Brightly colored yarn bobbins make it easy to grab the right strand when you need it.

Decorative scissors like these make you smile every time you use them.

Small, sharp scissors are a must.

Flat-headed pins in bright colors like these are fun to use.

This special ruler is useful for measuring stitches and rows in a gauge swatch.

Double-pronged pins work well with pieces made in bulky yarn.

Here's another variety of basting pin.

yarn resources

ALPACA WITH A TWIST
950 South White River
Parkway West Drive
Indianapolis, IN 46221
alpacawithatwist.com

ARTYARNS
39 Westmoreland Avenue
White Plains, NY 10606
artyarns.com

CARON INTERNATIONAL
P.O. Box 222
Washington, NC 27889
caron.com

CASCADE YARNS
1224 Andover Park East
Tukwila, WA 98188
cascadeyarns.com

CLASSIC ELITE YARNS
122 Western Avenue
Lowell, MA 01851
classiceliteyarns.com

COATS & CLARK
3430 Toringdon Way, Ste. 301
Charlotte, NC 28277
coatsandclark.com
In Canada:
6060 Burnside Court, Unit 2
Mississuaga, ON L5T 2T5

COLINETTE YARNS
Banwy Workshops
Llanfair Caereinion
Powys, SY210SG, U.K.
colinette.com

DMC
10 Basin Drive, Suite 130
Kearny, NJ 07032
www.dmc-usa.com

FAIRMOUNT FIBERS, INC.
915 North 28th Street
Philadelphia, PA 19130
fairmountfibers.com

FIBER TRENDS
P.O. Box 7266
East Wenatchee, WA 98802
fibertrends.com

FILATURA DI CROSA
dist. by Tahki•Stacy Charles,
Inc.

**THE GREAT ADIRONDACK
YARN CO.**
950 County Highway 126
Amsterdam, NY 12010

JCA, INC.
35 Scales Lane
Townsend, MA 01469
jcacrafts.com

JIL EATON COLLECTION
dist. by Classic Elite Yarns

LION BRAND YARN CO.
34 West 15th Street
New York, NY 10011
lionbrand.com

MANOS DEL URUGUAY
distributed by Fairmount
Fibers, Inc.
www.manos.com.uy

MODA DEA
distributed by Coats & Clark
modadea.com

NASHUA HANDKNITS
distributed by Westminster
Fibers, Inc.
nashuaknits.com

NATURALLY NZ
15 Church Street, Onehunga
Auckland, New Zealand
naturallyyarnsnz.com
In the U.S.:
distributed by Fiber Trends
In Canada:
distributed by The Old Mill
Knitting Co.

**THE OLD MILL KNITTING
CO.**
P.O. Box 81176
Ancaster, ON L9G 4X2
Canada
oldmillknitting.com

PATONS
320 Livingstone Ave. South
Listowel, ON N4W 3H3
Canada

PLYMOUTH YARN CO.
P.O. Box 28
Bristol, PA 19007
plymouthyarn.com

RED HEART
distributed by Coats & Clark

REYNOLDS
distributed by JCA, Inc.

ROWAN
dist. by Westminster Fibers
knitrowan.com

SCHOELLER+STAHL
dist. by Skacel Collection

SKACEL COLLECTION, INC.
P.O. Box 88110
Seattle, WA 98138
skacelknitting.com

TAHKI•STACY CHARLES, INC.
70-30 80th St., Building 36
Ridgewood, NY 11385
tahkistacycharles.com

TAHKI YARNS
dist. by Tahki•Stacy Charles

UNIVERSAL YARN
284 Ann Street
Concord, NC 28025
universalyarn.com

WESTMINSTER FIBERS, INC.
165 Ledge Street
Nashua, NH 03060
westminsterfibers.com

standard yarn weight system

Categories of yarn, gauge ranges,
and recommended needle and hook sizes

Yarn Weight Symbol & Category Names	(0) Lace	(1) Super Fine	(2) Fine	(3) Light	(4) Medium	(5) Bulky	(6) Super Bulky
Type of Yarns in Category	Fingering 10 count crochet thread	Sock, Fingering, Baby	Sport, Baby	DK, Light Worsted	Worsted, Afghan, Aran	Chunky, Craft, Rug	Bulky, Roving
Knit Gauge Range* in Stockinette Stitch to 4 inches	33–40** sts	27–32 sts	23–26 sts	21–24 sts	16–20 sts	12–15 sts	6–11 sts
Recommended Needle in Metric Size Range	1.5–2.25 mm	2.25–3.25 mm	3.25–3.75 mm	3.75–4.5 mm	4.5–5.5 mm	5.5–8 mm	8 mm and larger
Recommended Needle U.S. Size Range	000 to 1	1 to 3	3 to 5	5 to 7	7 to 9	9 to 11	11 and larger
Crochet Gauge* Ranges in Single Crochet to 4 inch	32–42 double crochets**	21–32 sts	16–20 sts	12–17 sts	11–14 sts	8–11 sts	5–9 sts
Recommended Hook in Metric Size Range	Steel*** 1.6–1.4mm Regular hook 2.25 mm	2.25–3.5 mm	3.5–4.5 mm	4.5–5.5 mm	5.5–6.5 mm	6.5–9 mm	9 mm and larger
Recommended Hook U.S. Size Range	Steel*** 6, 7, 8 Regular hook B–1	B–1 to E–4	E–4 to 7	7 to I–9	I–9 to K–10½	K–10½ to M–13	M–13 and larger

* GUIDELINES ONLY: The above reflect the most commonly used gauges and needle or hook sizes for specific yarn categories.

** Lace weight yarns are usually knitted or crocheted on larger needles and hooks to create lacy, openwork patterns. Accordingly, a gauge range is difficult to determine. Always follow the gauge stated in your pattern.

*** Steel crochet hooks are sized differently from regular hooks—the higher the number, the smaller the hook, which is the reverse of regular hook sizing.

KNIT HOW the basics of knitting: getting started

Whether you're a knitting novice or just need to brush up on the basics, this quick refresher course will get you clicking.

slipknot

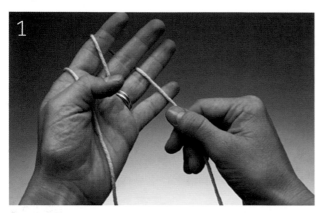

The slipknot becomes the first stitch. Hold the tail end of the yarn in your palm with your thumb. Wrap the yarn from the ball twice around your index and middle fingers.

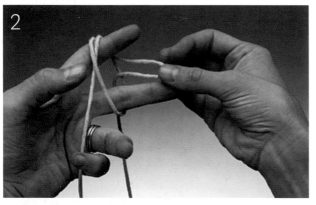

Pull the strand attached to the ball through the loop between your two fingers to form a new loop.

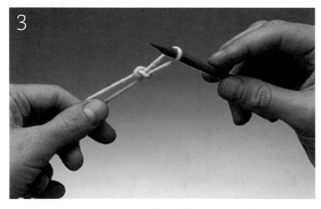

Place the new loop on the needle. Tighten it by pulling on both ends of the yarn to form the slipknot. To prepare for casting on, leave an extra-long tail when making the slipknot.

casting on

With a slipknot on the needle in your right hand, wind the tail end around your left thumb. Wrap yarn from the ball over your left index finger. Hold both ends in your palm.

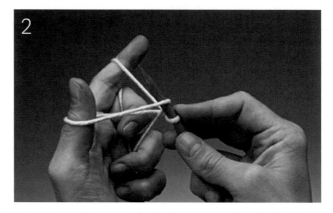

Insert the needle upward in the loop on your thumb, then behind the loop on your index finger. Use the needle to draw the yarn up from the ball through the loop to form a stitch.

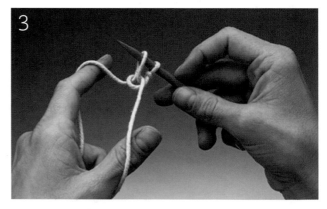

Take your thumb out of the loop and pull the tail end to tighten the stitch on the needle. Repeat Steps 1 to 3 until the desired number of stitches is cast on.

making a knit stitch

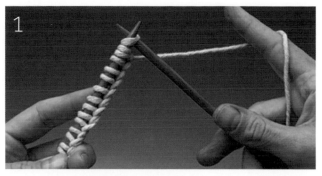

1

The needle with the stitches is in your left hand, the first stitch near the tip. With the empty needle in your right hand, wrap the yarn around your fingers as shown. Insert the right needle from front to back into the first stitch on the left needle. Keep the right needle under the left needle and the yarn at the back.

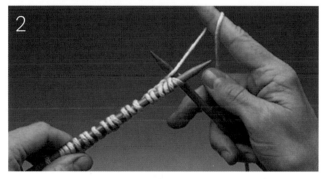

2

Bring the yarn under and over the right needle, and pull it gently between the two needles. Use your right index finger to manipulate the yarn.

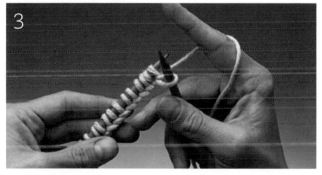

3

With the right needle, catch the yarn and pull it through the stitch on the left needle.

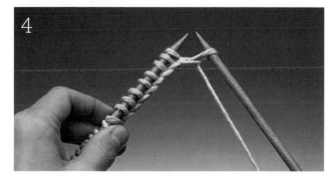

4

Slip the stitch off the left needle, leaving the new stitch on the right. Repeat Steps 1 to 4 until all the new stitches are on the right needle.

making a purl stitch

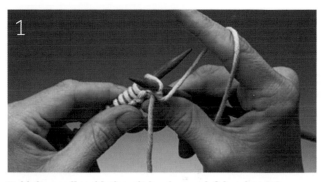

1

Hold the needle with the stitches in your left hand and the empty needle in your right hand. For the purl stitch, the yarn is held to the front of the work. Insert the right needle from back to front into the first stitch. The right needle is in front of the left needle, and the yarn is at the front of your work.

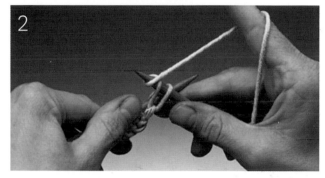

2

With your right index finger, wrap the yarn counterclockwise around the right needle, as shown.

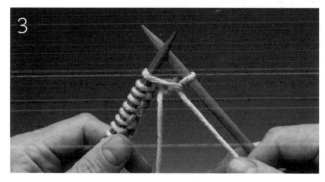

3

Draw the right needle and yarn backwards through the stitch on the left needle, forming a loop on the right needle.

4

Slip the stitch off the left needle. Repeat steps 1 to 4 until all the new stitches are on the right needle.

KNIT HOW the basics of crochet: getting started

There's no substitute for a hands-on teacher, but our step-by-step primer is the next best thing. So pick up a hook and some yarn, get yourself comfortably seated and let the fun begin!

slipknot

Make a loop, placing one end of the yarn centered underneath the loop. Insert the hook under the center strand and pull it up into a loop on the hook. Pull both yarn ends to tighten the knot on the hook.

single crochet

Make a foundation chain of desired length. Insert the hook under 2 loops of the next chain stitch and yarn over. (On a foundation row, start in the second chain from the hook.)

foundation chain

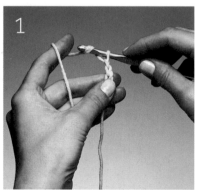

Place the head of the hook under the long end of the yarn. The yarn should lie over the hook from back to front. This is called "yarn over."

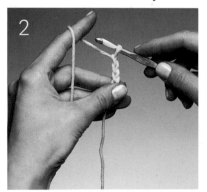

Pull the yarn-over through the loop already on the hook—one chain has been completed.

slip stitch

Insert the hook under both of the top 2 loops of the next stitch and yarn over.

Draw the yarn-over through the stitch and the loop on the hook in one motion.

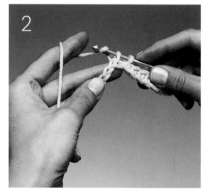

Draw the yarn-over through the chain, then yarn over once again. (There are now 2 loops on the hook plus the new yarn-over.)

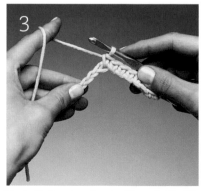

Draw the new yarn-over through the 2 loops on the hook—one single crochet completed.

half double crochet

To begin a half double crochet stitch, yarn over.

Insert hook under the 2 top loops of the next stitch and yarn over.

Draw yarn-over through stitch; yarn over again.

Draw yarn-over through all 3 loops on hook—one half double crochet completed.

double crochet

To begin a double crochet stitch, yarn over.

Insert hook under the 2 top loops of the next stitch and yarn over once again.

Draw the yarn-over through the stitch—3 loops are on hook; yarn over once again.

Draw yarn-over through first 2 loops; yarn over once again. Draw yarn-over through last 2 loops on hook to complete double crochet.

Chart Toppers

d

e

f

Shuffle your playlist
with our rockin' hat pattern
and its endless options.

Designed by John Brinegar
Photographs by Jenny Acheson

j

k

l

Chart Toppers cont.

MATERIALS

Zara by Filatura Di Crosa/Tahki•Stacy Charles, Inc., 1¾oz/50g balls, each approx 137yd/125m (merino wool)

- **One set (5) each size 5 and 6 (3.75 and 4mm) double-pointed needles (dpns) OR SIZE TO OBTAIN GAUGE**

Zara Plus by Filatura Di Crosa/Tahki•Stacy Charles, Inc., 1¾oz/50g balls, each approx 77yd/70m (merino wool)

- **One set (5) each size 7 and 8 (4.5 and 5mm) double-pointed needles (dpns) OR SIZE TO OBTAIN GAUGE**

Torino Bulky by Filatura Di Crosa/Tahki•Stacy Charles, Inc., 1¾oz/50g balls, each approx 55yd/50m (merino wool)

- **One set (5) each size 9 and 10 (5.5 and 6mm) double-pointed needles (dpns) OR SIZE TO OBTAIN GAUGE**

●●○○

Sized to fit Preemie (12"/30.5cm), Baby (14"/35.5cm), Toddler (16"/40.5cm), Child (18"/45.5cm), Woman (20"/50.5cm), Man (22"/56cm). All hats shown in size Child (18"/45.5cm).

GAUGES

- 23 sts and 32 rnds to 4"/10cm over St st using Zara and size 6 (4mm) needles.
- 19 sts and 27 rnds to 4"/10cm over St st using Zara Plus and size 8 (5mm) needles.
- 16 sts and 23 rnds to 4"/10cm over St st using Torino Bulky and size 10 (6mm) needles.

TAKE TIME TO CHECK YOUR GAUGES.

NOTES

There are two basic hat styles, one in St st and one in k2, p2 ribbing. Three different yarn weights have been used. All variations of the basic hats are given below and can be mixed and matched as desired. Follow the basic hat pattern, using the chart on page 27 for the specific sts and measurements for the desired size and gauge. The details for each hat shown (styles A–L) are also given.

BRIM STYLES

Ribbed Brim

Work in k2, p2 rib for 1 (1, 1, 1½, 1½,1½)"/2.5 (2.5, 2.5, 4, 4, 4)cm.

Turn up Ribbed Brim

Work in k2, p2 rib for 2 (2, 2, 3, 3, 3)"/6.5 (6.5, 6.5, 7.5, 7.5, 7.5)cm.

Garter Brim

Work in garter st for ½ (¾, ¾, 1, 1, 1)"/1.5 (2, 2, 2.5, 2.5, 2.5)cm.

Rolled Brim

Work in St st for 1 (1, 1, 1½, 1½,1½)"/2.5 (2.5, 2.5, 4, 4, 4)cm. Allow to curl.

BASIC HAT PATTERN

BRIM

Following chart appropriate for desired gauge and hat size, with smaller needles, cast on the number of sts indicated on chart. Divide sts evenly over 4 needles. Place marker and join for knitting in the round, being careful not to twist sts. Work in desired brim style.

HAT

Cont in k2, p2 rib (for ribbed version) OR change to larger needles and work in St st for "length to dec" as indicated on chart.

Crown shaping (St st version)

Note For *Zara Plus* version, sizes Baby and Toddler *only*, begin with rnd 5.

a   b   c

d   e   f

Rnd 1 *K2tog, K6; rep from * around.
Rnd 2 and all even-numbered rnds Work in pat as established.
Rnd 3 *K2tog, k5; rep from * around.
Rnd 5 *K2tog, k4; rep from * around.
Rnd 7 *K2tog, k3; rep from * around.
Rnd 9 *K2tog, k2; rep from * around.
Rnd 11 *K2tog, k1; rep from * around.
Rnd 13 *K2tog; rep from * around.
Cut yarn, leaving a 12"/30.5cm tail, thread through rem sts, cinch tightly to close. Add pompoms and/or earflaps as desired.

Crown shaping (ribbed version)
Note For *Torino Bulky* version, work rnds 1–7 *only*.
Rnd 1 *K2, p2tog; rep from * to end.
Work 3 rnds even.
Rnd 5 *K2tog, p1; rep from * to end.
Work 2 rnds even.
Rnd 8 *K2tog, p2tog; rep from * to end.
Work 1 rnd even.
Rnd 10 *K2tog; rep from * to end.
Cut yarn, leaving a 12"/30.5cm tail, thread through rem sts, cinch tightly to close. Add pompoms and/or earflaps as desired.

Earflaps
Lay hat flat, and place markers at one-third intervals, dividing each side of hat into 3 sections. With smaller needles, working between the markers, pick up and knit sts as indicated on chart along cast-on edge of hat. Work earflaps in garter st, following chart for length. Decrease 1 st at beg of every row following chart for the number of times. Bind off remaining sts or continue to dec until there are 3 sts, then work I-cord as foll:
*Next row (RS) Knit 3. Do *not* turn. Slide sts to beg of needle to knit next row on RS. Rep from * to desired length.

HAT A
- 2 balls of *Zara Plus* in #17 orange (A)
- 1 ball in #409 lime green (B)

Following chart for desired gauge and size, with smaller needles and A, cast on __ sts. Work garter brim style. Change to larger needles. Work in St st for length given in chart. Work crown shaping.

Earflaps
Mark cast-on edge for earflaps. Following chart for desired gauge and size, with smaller needles and B, pick up and knit __ sts. Work in garter st for length given in chart. Dec 1 st at beg of every row __ times. Bind off rem sts. Rep for other side.

Pompom
With B, make a 2"/5cm pompom and attach it to top of hat.

HAT B
- 1 ball each of *Torino Bulky* in #219 olive (A) and #211 navy (B)

With smaller needles and A, cast on __ sts. Work rolled brim style. Change to larger needles and B, work in rev St st for ½"/1.5cm. Change to A, work in St st for length given in chart. Change to B and work crown shaping.

HAT C
- 2 balls of *Zara* in #1401 white (A)
- 1 ball in #1473 turquoise (B)

With smaller needles and A, cast on __ sts. Work garter brim style. Change to larger needles and St st for length given in chart. Work crown shaping.

Earflaps
Mark cast-on edge for earflaps. Following chart for desired gauge and size, with smaller needles and B, pick up and knit __ sts. Work following chart for length and work in garter st and stripe pat as foll: *2 rows B, 2 rows A; rep from * for stripe pat. Dec 1 st at beg of every row until there are 3 sts. Work I-cord for 5"/12.5cm or desired length. Rep on other side. With B, make a 2"/5cm pompon and attach it to top of hat. With A, make two 2"/5cm pompoms and attach them to I-cord on earflaps.

HAT D
- 1 ball each of *Torino Bulky* in #211 navy (A), #203 tan (B) and #216 olive green (C).

With smaller needles and A, cast on __ sts. Work in k2, p2 rib as foll: *3 rows A, 4 rows B, 4 rows C, 4 rows A; rep from * throughout and work even for length given in chart. Work crown shaping.

HAT E
- 1 ball each of *Zara* in #1473 turquoise (A) and #1731 rust (B)

With smaller needles and A, cast on __ sts. Work ribbed brim style. Change to larger needles. Work in St st, for length given in chart. Work crown shaping.

Pompom
With B, make a 2"/5cm pompom and attach it to top of hat.

HAT F
- 2 balls of *Torino Bulky* in #203 tan (A)
- 1 ball in #216 olive (B)

With smaller needles and A, cast on __ sts. Work ribbed brim style. Change to larger needles. Work in St st for length given in chart. Work crown shaping.

Pompom
With B, make a 2"/5cm pompom and attach it to top of hat.

Chart Toppers cont.

HAT G
- 2 balls of *Zara* in #1666 magenta (A)
- 1 ball in #1404 black (B)

With smaller needles and B, cast on __ sts. Work 2 rnds with B in turn up ribbed brim style. Change to A and complete turn up ribbed brim style. Change to larger needles. Work in St st for length given in chart. Work crown shaping.

HAT H
- 1 ball each of *Zara Plus* in #21 turquoise (A), #2 white (B) and #409 lime green (C)

With smaller needles and A, cast on __ sts. Work in k2, p2 rib and stripe pat as foll: *4 rnds A, 2 rnds B, 8 rnds C, 2 rnds A, 6 rnds B, 2 rnds C; rep from * for stripe pat throughout. Work even for length given in chart. Work crown shaping.

HAT I
- 2 balls of *Zara Plus* in #409 lime green (A)
- 1 ball in #22 magenta (B)

With smaller needles and A, cast on __ sts. Work ribbed brim style. Change to larger needles. Work in St st for length given in chart. Work crown shaping.

Pompom
With B, make a 2"/5cm pompom and attach it to top of hat.

HAT J
- 1 ball each of *Zara Plus* in #2 white (A) and #17 orange (B)

Check Stitch Pattern
Rnd 1 *K 1 A, k 1 B; rep from * to end.
Rnd 2 *K 1 B, k 1 A; rep from * to end.
Rep rnds 1 and 2 for Check Stitch Pattern.
With smaller needles and A, cast on __ sts. Work rolled brim style. Change to larger needles. Work in St st and work 7

rnds in check stitch pat. Continue in St st with A for length given in chart. Change to B and work crown shaping.

Pompom
With A, make a 2"/5cm pompom and attach it to top of hat.

HAT K
- 1 ball each of *Zara* in #1666 magenta (A) and #1727 green (B)

With smaller needles and A, cast on __ sts. Work in k2, p2 rib and stripes as foll: *13 rnds A, 13 rnds B; rep from * for stripe pat throughout. Work even for length given in chart. Work crown shaping.

HAT L
- 2 balls of *Torino Bulky* in #211 navy (A)
- 1 ball in #203 tan (B)
- One size I/9 (5.5mm) crochet hook

With smaller needles and A, cast on __ sts. Work garter brim style. Change to larger needles. Work in St st for length given in chart. Work crown shaping.

Earflaps
Mark cast-on edge for earflaps. Following chart for desired gauge and size, with smaller needles and A, pick up and knit __ sts. Work in garter st for length given in chart. Dec 1 st at beg of every row __ times. Bind off rem sts. Rep for other side.

Crochet edging
With crochet hook and B, beg at back of hat and work 1 sc in each st around and work 2 sc in each bottom corner of earflaps. ✿

g   h   i

j   k   l

Zara, 6 (4mm) needles, 23 stitches & 32 rows to 4"/10cm

Size	Preemie	Baby	Toddler	Child	Woman	Man
Finished measurement	12½"/31.5cm	14"/35.5cm	16¾"/42.5cm	18"/45.5cm	20¾"/52.5cm	22¼"/56.5cm
Cast on _ stitches	72	80	96	104	120	128
Length to decrease	2½"/6.5cm	3"/7.5cm	3"/7.5cm	3½"/9cm	3½"/9cm	4"/10cm
Earflaps						
Pick-up _ stitches	12	16	20	24	24	24
Length to decrease	¾"/2cm	1"/2.5cm	1"/2.5cm	1½"/4cm	1½"/4cm	1½"/4cm
Decrease _ times	8	10	12	14	14	14

Zara Plus, 8 (5mm) needles, 19 stitches & 27 rows to 4"/10cm

Size	Preemie	Baby	Toddler	Child	Woman	Man
Finished measurement	11¾"/30cm	13¾"/35cm	16½"/42cm	18½"/47cm	20¼"/51.5cm	22"/56cm
Cast on _ stitches	56	66	78	88	96	104
Length to decrease	2½"/6.5cm	3"/7.5cm	3"/7.5cm	3½"/9cm	3½"/9cm	4"/10cm
Earflaps						
Pick-up _ stitches	10	14	18	20	20	20
Length to decrease	¾"/2cm	1"/2.5cm	1"/2.5cm	1½"/4cm	1½"/4cm	1½"/4cm
Decrease _ times	8	10	12	12	12	12

Torino Bulky, 10 (6mm) needles, 16 stitches & 23 rows to 4"/10cm

Size	Preemie	Baby	Toddler	Child	Woman	Man
Finished measurement	12"/30.5cm	14"/35.5cm	16"/40.5cm	18"/45.5cm	20"/50.5cm	22"/56cm
Cast on _ stitches	48	56	64	72	80	88
Length to decrease	2½"/6.5cm	3"/7.5cm	3"/7.5cm	3½"/9cm	3½"/9cm	4"/10cm
Earflaps						
Pick-up _ stitches	8	10	14	14	16	16
Length to decrease	¾"/2cm	1"/2.5cm	1"/2.5cm	1½"/4cm	1½"/4cm	1½"/4cm
Decrease _ times	6	8	10	10	10	10

Start with one versatile pattern, end up with five adorable sets of handwarmers. Talk about a perfectly portable project!

Smitten With Mittens

MATERIALS

TLC Essentials by Coats & Clark, 6oz/170g skeins, each approx 312yd/285m (acrylic)
- **1 skein in desired color**
- **Five size 6 (4mm) dp needles, OR SIZE TO OBTAIN GAUGE**
- **Small stitch holder (optional)**

●●○○

Designed by Charlotte Parry
Photographs by Paul Amato

Basic mitten sized for children, women, men.

FINISHED MEASUREMENTS
- Length from wrist to fingertips 7 (10, 11)"/18 (25.5, 28)cm
- Wrist circumference 5¼ (6½, 7½)"/13.5 (16.5, 19)cm

GAUGE
20 sts and 28 rows to 4"/10cm over St st using size 6 (4mm) needles. TAKE TIME TO CHECK YOUR GAUGE.

LEFT MITTEN
Cast on 8 (10, 12) sts on first dpn, 8 (10, 12) sts on 2nd dpn, 8 (10, 12) sts on 3rd dpn and 8 (10, 12) sts on 4th dpn—32 (40, 48) sts. Pm to mark beg of rnd and join. Work in k1, p1 rib for 2 (3, 3)"/5 (7.5, 7.5)cm. Change to St st and work even for 3 rows.

Base of thumb shaping
Rnd 1 K12 (16, 20), M1, k2, M1, k rem sts to end—34 (42, 50) sts. **Rnds 2 and 3** Knit. **Rnd 4** K12 (16, 20), M1, k4, M1, k rem sts to end—36 (44, 52) sts. **Rnds 5 and 6** Knit. **Rnd 7** K12 (16, 20), M1, k6, M1, k rem sts to end—38 (46, 54) sts. **Rnds 8 and 9** Knit. **Rnd 10** K12 (16, 20), M1, k8, M1, k rem sts to end—40 (48, 56) sts. **Rnds 11 and 12** Knit. **Rnd 13** K12 (16, 20), M1, k10, M1, k rem sts to end—42 (50, 58) sts.

For women's and men's sizes only
Rnds 14 and 15 Knit. **Rnd 16** K (16, 20), M1, k12, M1, k rem sts to end—(52, 60) sts. **Rnd 17** Knit.

For men's size only
Rnds 18 and 19 Knit. **Rnd 20** K20, M1, k14, M1, k rem sts to end—62 sts. **Rnd 21** Knit.

For all sizes
Next rnd K12 (16, 20), place next 12 (14, 16) sts on a holder (either a contrast color strand of yarn or a small stitch holder) for thumb, cast on 2 sts, k to end of rnd—32 (40, 48) sts.
Cont in St st on 32 (40, 48) sts for hand of mitten until piece is 5½ (8½, 9½)"/14 (21.5, 24)cm, or until hand is long enough to cover index fingernail.

Mitten top shaping
Rnd 1 K1, SKP, k10 (14, 18), k2tog, k2, SKP, k10 (14, 18), k2tog, k1—28 (36, 44) sts.
Rnd 2 K1, SKP, k8 (12, 16), k2tog, k2, SKP, k8 (12, 16) sts, k2tog, k1—24 (32, 40) sts.
Rnd 3 K1, SKP, k6 (10, 14), k2tog, k2, SKP, k6 (10, 14), k2tog, k1—20 (28, 36) sts.
Rnd 4 K1, SKP, k4 (8, 12), k2tog, k2, SKP, k4 (8, 12), k2tog, k1—16 (24, 32) sts.
Rnd 5 K1, SKP, k2 (6, 10), k2tog, k2, SKP, k2 (6, 10), k2tog, k1—12 (20, 28) sts.
For women's and men's sizes only
Rnd 6 K1, SKP, k(4, 8), k2tog, k2, SKP, k(4, 8), k2tog, k1—(16, 24) sts.

Rnd 7 K1, SKP, k(2, 6), k2tog, k2, SKP, k(2, 6), k2tog, k1—(12, 20) sts.

For men's size only

Rnd 8 K1, SKP, k4, k2tog, k2, SKP, k4, k2tog, k1—16 sts.

Rnd 9 K1, SKP, k2, k2tog, k2, SKP, k2, k2tog, k1—12 sts.

For all sizes

Last rnd K1, SKP, k2tog, k2, SKP, k2tog, k1—8 sts.

Cut yarn, draw yarn end through rem 8 sts and fasten off.

THUMB

Pick up 5 (6, 7) sts from 12 (14, 16) sts on holder with first dpn, 5 (6, 7) sts with 2nd dpn and 2 sts with 3rd dpn; pick up and knit 2 sts from hand of mitten—14 (16, 18) sts.

Work even in St st until thumb measures 1¼ (2, 2¼)"/3.5 (5, 6)cm, or long enough to cover half of thumbnail.

Next row [K2tog, k1] 4 (5, 6) times, k2 (1, 0)—10 (11, 12) sts.

Next row [K2 tog] 5 (5, 6) times, k0 (1, 0)— 5 (6, 6) sts.

Next row [K2 tog] 2 (3, 3) times, k1 (0, 0)—3 sts.

Cut yarn, draw yarn end through rem 3 sts and fasten off.

RIGHT MITTEN

Work as for left mitten except position base of thumb as follows:

Rnd 1 K18 (22, 26), M1, k2, M1, k rem sts to end—34 (42, 50) sts.

Shape remainder of thumb base and mitten as for left mitten. ✿

1

2

3

1. Knitting mittens in rounds on 4 needles (plus 1 working needle) eliminates the need for most seaming. Work the ribbing first, followed by increases up to the base of the thumb. Place the thumb sts on a holder—either a strand of yarn or a safety pin will do.

2. Stitches are decreased to shape the top of the mitten. Work slip 1, knit 1, pass the slip stitch over (SKP) to slant the decrease line to the left; knit 2 stitches together (k2tog) to angle the decrease line to the right. When all decreases are made, cut the yarn and thread it through the remaining stitches, pull tightly to gather and fasten off.

3. To knit the thumb, divide the stitches between 3 needles and pick up and knit a few stitches on the hand of the mitten to avoid creating a hole. To get a good fit, knit in rounds until the piece covers half the thumbnail. Then, work the final decreases and close as for top of mitten.

ESSENTIALS

The argyle pattern on this fun Fair Isle duo is embroidered on after knitting using duplicate stitch.

The New Argyle

MATERIALS

TLC Essentials by Coats & Clark, 6oz/170g skeins, each approx 312yd/285m (acrylic)
- **1 skein each in #2915 cranberry (MC), #2772 rose and #2316 winter white**
- **Five size 6 (4mm) dp needles, OR SIZE TO OBTAIN GAUGE**
- **Safety pin or small stitch holder**

●●○○

Designed by Charlotte Parry
Photographs by Paul Amato

Basic argyle mitten sized for children, women, men. Shown in women's size.

FINISHED MEASUREMENTS
- Length from wrist to fingertips 7 (10, 11)"/18 (25.5, 28)cm
- Wrist circumference 5¼ (6½, 7½)"/13.5 (16.5, 19)cm

GAUGE
20 sts and 28 rows to 4"/10cm over St st using size 6 (4mm) needles.
TAKE TIME TO CHECK YOUR GAUGE

MITTENS
With MC, work as for basic mittens on pages 28–29. The argyle pattern can be embroidered by centering the 11-stitch chart on the back of each mitten. Work as many reps of the argyle chart as necessary for each size, ending with a row 7. ✪

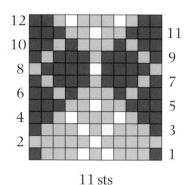

11 sts

COLOR KEY

■ Cranberry
□ Winter white
■ Rose

Line It Up

MATERIALS

TLC Essentials by Coats & Clark, 6oz/170g skeins, each approx 312yd/285m (acrylic)

- **1 skein each in #2915 cranberry (A), #2855 navy (B), #2918 harvest (C)**
- **Five size 6 (4mm) dp needles, OR SIZE TO OBTAIN GAUGE**
- **Safety pin or small stitch holder**

●●○○○

Designed by Charlotte Parry
Photographs by Paul Amato

Basic wide striped mitten sized for children, women, men. Shown in women's size.

FINISHED MEASUREMENTS

- Length from wrist to fingertips 7 (10, 11)"/18 (25.5, 28)cm
- Wrist circumference 5¼ (6½, 7½)"/13.5 (16.5, 19)cm

GAUGE

20 sts and 28 rows to 4"/10cm over St st using size 6 (4mm) needles. TAKE TIME TO CHECK YOUR GAUGE.

MITTENS

Work as for basic mitten on pages 28–29. Work ribbing with A; work hand in alternating 6-row stripes of B and C; work top portion of thumb with A. ✪

Jazzy Bands

MATERIALS

TLC Essentials by Coats & Clark, 6oz/170g skeins, each approx 312yd/285m (acrylic)

- **1 skein each in #2254 persimmon (A) and #2220 butter (B)**
- **Five size 6 (4mm) dp needles, OR SIZE TO OBTAIN GAUGE**
- **Safety pin or small stitch holder**

●●○○○

Designed by Charlotte Parry
Photographs by Paul Amato

Basic two-striped mitten sized for children, women, men. Shown in women's size.

FINISHED MEASUREMENTS

- Length from wrist to fingertips 7 (10, 11)"/18 (25.5, 28)cm
- Wrist circumference 5¼ (6½, 7½)"/13.5 (16.5, 19)cm

GAUGE

20 sts and 28 rows to 4"/10cm over St st using size 6 (4mm) needles. TAKE TIME TO CHECK YOUR GAUGE.

MITTENS

Work as for basic mittens on pages 28–29, but work entire piece in a 2-row alternating stripe pattern of A and B. ✪

Block Party

MATERIALS

TLC Essentials by Coats & Clark, 6oz/170g skeins, each approx 312yd/285m (acrylic)

- **1 skein each in #2313 aran (A), #2673 medium thyme (B), #2220 butter (C) and #2254 persimmon (D)**
- **Five size 6 (4mm) dp needles, OR SIZE TO OBTAIN GAUGE**
- **Safety pin or small stitch holder**

●●○○○

Designed by Charlotte Parry
Photographs by Paul Amato

Basic colorblocked mitten sized for children, women, men. Shown in women's size.

FINISHED MEASUREMENTS

- Length from wrist to fingertips 7 (10, 11)"/18 (25.5, 28)cm
- Wrist circumference 5¼ (6½, 7½)"/13.5 (16.5, 19)cm

GAUGE

20 sts and 28 rows to 4"/10cm over St st using size 6 (4mm) needles. TAKE TIME TO CHECK YOUR GAUGE.

MITTENS

Work as for basic mittens on pages 28–29. Work rib with A; 28 rnds of hand and up to base of thumb with B; remainder of hand with C and top of thumb with D. ✪

Line It Up

Jazzy Bands

Block Party

ESSENTIALS

Success pops up under your thumb when you adapt our basic mitten for fit and fancy.

Quite a Handful

MATERIALS
Renaissance by Classic Elite Yarns, 1¾oz/50g skeins, each approx 110yd/100m (wool)
- **One set (5) size 6 (4mm) double-pointed needles (dpns) OR SIZE TO OBTAIN GAUGE**

Bazic Wool by Classic Elite Yarns, 1¾oz/50g balls, each approx 65yd/59m (superwash wool)
- **One set (5) size 8 (5mm) double-pointed needles (dpns) OR SIZE TO OBTAIN GAUGE**

Paintbox by Classic Elite Yarns, 1¾oz/50g balls, each approx 110yd/100m (merino wool)
- **One set (5) size 10 (6mm) double-pointed needles (dpns) OR SIZE TO OBTAIN GAUGE**

Sinful by Classic Elite Yarns, 1¾oz/50g balls, each approx 65yd/59m (merino wool)
- **One set (5) size 10 (6mm) double-pointed needles (dpns) OR SIZE TO OBTAIN GAUGE**
- **Stitch markers and holder**

●●○○

Designed by Linda Cyr
Photographs by Marcus Tullis

Sized for Man (Woman, Child).

MEASUREMENTS
- **Palm** 9 (7½. 6)"/23 (19, 15)cm
- **Length** 11½ (9½, 7)"/29 (24, 17.5)cm

GAUGES
- 19 sts and 27 rnds to 4"/10cm over St st using Renaissance and size 6 (4mm) needles.
- 16 sts and 24 rnds to 4"/10cm over St st using Bazic Wool and size 8 (5mm) needles.
- 14 sts and 17 rnds to 4"/10cm over St st using Paintbox and size 10 (6mm) needles.
- 14 sts and 17 rnds to 4"/10cm over St st using Sinful and size 10 (6mm) needles. TAKE TIME TO CHECK YOUR GAUGES.

NOTES
1) When changing colors in ribbing, always work first rnd of new color in St st.

2) When making paired incs for the thumbs, make the first inc by knitting into the st below the next st on the L needle, make second inc by knitting into the st 2 sts below the st just knit.

3) Some sizes work shaping differently on some rows. Look for the * in the pattern and on the chart on page 38.

Basic Mitten Pattern

Using chart appropriate for your chosen size and yarn to fill in blanks, cast on __ sts. Divide on dpns, place marker and join for knitting in the round. Work in k2, p2 rib for __"/__cm. Change to St st and work even until piece measures __"/__ from ribbing.

Next rnd K__, M1, k__, M1, pm, k to end. Work 2 rnds even.

Next rnd K__, M1, k to marker, M1, sl m, k to end. Work 2 rnds even. Rep last 3 rnds __ times.

Next rnd K__, cast on __, sl __ sts to holder, k to end. Work 2 rnds even.

Next rnd * K__, ssk, k__, k2tog, k to end. Work 2 rnds even.

Next rnd * K__, ssk, k2tog, k to end. Work __ rnds even.

Next rnd [K2, k2tog, k__, ssk, pm, k__] twice. Work 2 rnds even.

Next (dec) rnd K2, k2tog, k to 2 sts before marker, ssk, sl m, k __. Work 1 rnd even. Rep last 2 rnds __ times. Rep dec rnd __ times. Graft or sew rem sts together.

Thumb

Pick up 1 st each side of thumb opening and __ sts along cast-on edge. K across __ sts from holder.

decreases

mitt

embroidery

side stitch

thumb

gusset

cuff

Quite a Handful cont.

Next rnd K1, ssk, k__, k2tog, k to end. Work 1 rnd.
Next rnd * K1, ssk, k2tog, k around. K __ rnds even.
Cut yarn with an 8"/20.5cm tail, thread through rem sts and cinch tightly to close.

MITTEN A (shown in Man's size)
MATERIALS
• 1 skein each of Renaissance in #7191 blue (A) and #7172 green (B)
• One set (5) size 8 (5mm) dpns OR SIZE TO OBTAIN GAUGE
MITTEN
Following Basic Mitten Pattern and chart for chosen size, begin mitten in A and work until 15 rnds completed over ribbing, work 2 rnds in B, 2 rnds in A, 19 rnds in B, 2 rnds in A, 2 rnds in B, finish with A. Work thumb to correspond.

MITTEN B (shown in Women's size)
MATERIALS
• 1 skein each of Renaissance in #7191 blue (A) and #7172 green (B)
• One set (5) size 8 (5mm) dpns OR SIZE TO OBTAIN GAUGE
MITTEN
Following Basic Mitten Pattern and chart for chosen size, begin mitten in A and work until 2 rnds completed, finish in B. With A, duplicate st Snowflake chart onto backs of mittens.

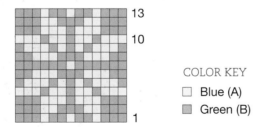

COLOR KEY
□ Blue (A)
▨ Green (B)

MITTEN C (shown in Child's size)
MATERIALS
• 1 skein each of Renaissance in #7172 green (A) and #7191 blue (B)
• One set (5) size 8 (5mm) dpns OR SIZE TO OBTAIN GAUGE
MITTEN
Following Basic Mitten Pattern and chart for chosen size, begin mitten in A and work until ribbing is completed, finish with B. With 2 strands of A, tapestry needle and chain st, embroider hearts on backs of mittens.

MITTEN D (shown in Man's size)
MATERIALS
• 1 ball each of Bazic Wool in #2972 green (A) and #2914 wedgewood blue (B)

• One set (5) size 8 (5mm) dpns OR SIZE TO OBTAIN GAUGE
MITTEN
Following Basic Mitten Pattern and chart for chosen size, begin mitten in A and work until 2 rnds completed, work in B until 17 rnds completed above ribbing, work [3 rnds in A, 2 rnds in B] four times, 3 rnds in A, finish in B. Work thumb to correspond.

MITTEN E (shown in Woman's size)
MATERIALS
• 1 ball each of Bazic Wool in #2972 green (A) and #2914 wedgewood blue (B)
• One set (5) size 8 (5mm) dpns OR SIZE TO OBTAIN GAUGE
MITTEN
Following Basic Mitten Pattern and chart for chosen size, begin mitten in A and work until ribbing is completed, finish with B. With A and using photo for reference, embroider flowers on backs of mittens with 5 lazy daisy petals and a large French knot center.

MITTEN F (shown in Child's size)
MATERIALS
• 1 ball each of Bazic Wool in #2914 wedgewood blue (A) and #2972 green (B)
• One set (5) size 8 (5mm) dpns OR SIZE TO OBTAIN GAUGE
MITTEN
Following Basic Mitten Pattern and chart for chosen size, begin mitten in A and work until rib is completed, work [4 rnds B and 1 rnd A] to end of mitten. Work thumb to correspond.

MITTEN G (shown in Man's size)
MATERIALS
• 2 balls of Paintbox in #6857 blue
• One set (5) size 10 (6mm) dpns OR SIZE TO OBTAIN GAUGE
MITTEN
Follow Basic Mitten Pattern and chart for chosen size.

MITTEN H (shown in Woman's size)
MATERIALS
• 2 balls of Sinful in #20591 blue
• One set (5) size 10 (6mm) dpns OR SIZE TO OBTAIN GAUGE
MITTEN
Follow Basic Mitten Pattern and chart for chosen size.

MITTEN I (shown in Child's size)
MATERIALS
• 2 balls of Paintbox in #6897 green
• One set (5) size 10 (6mm) dpns OR SIZE TO OBTAIN GAUGE
MITTEN
Follow Basic Mitten Pattern and chart for chosen size. ✪

a

b

c

d

e

f

g

h

i

Quite a Handful CHART cont.

Instructions / Directions	DK Man	DK Woman	DK Child	Worsted Man	Worsted Woman	Worsted Child	Bulky Man	Bulky Woman	Bulky Child
Cast on __ sts	44	36	28	36	32	24	32	28	20
Rib for __"/__ cm	2¾/7	2¼/5.5	1¾/4.5	2¾/7	2¼/5.5	1¾/4.5	2¾/7	2¼/5.5	1¾/4.5
St st for __"/__ cm	¾/2	¾/2	½/1.5	¾/2	¾/2	½/1.5	¾/2	¾/2	½/1.5
K__, M1	20	16	13	16	14	11	15	13	9
K__, M1, pm, k to end. Work 2 rnds even.	4	4	3	4	4	3	4	4	3
K__, M1, k to marker, m1, sl marker, k to end. Work 2 rnds even.	20	16	13	16	14	11	15	13	9
Rep last 3 rnds __ times.	4	3	2	3	3	2	3	2	1
K__,	21	17	14	17	15	12	16	14	10
Cast on __,	6	6	5	6	6	5	5	5	5
Sl__ sts to holder, k to end. Work 2 rnds even.	12	10	7	10	10	7	9	7	5
K__, ssk.	21	17	14	17	15	12	16	14	10
K__, k2tog, k to end. Work 2 rnds even.	2	2	1	2	2	1	1	1	1
K__, ssk, k2tog, k to end.	21	17	14*	17	15	12*	16*	14*	10*
Work __ rnds even.	16	12	7	16	12	8	5	4	1
[K2, k2tog, k __, ssk, pm,	14	10	7	10	8	5	9	7	3
k __] twice. Work 2 rnds even.	2	2	1	2	2	1	1	1	1
K2, k2tog, k to 2 sts before marker, ssk, sl marker, k __ (dec rnd). Work 1 rnd even.	2	2	1	2	2	0	1	1	1
Rep last 2 rnds __ times.	3	2	1	2	1	1	1	1	0
Rep dec rnd __ times.	3	2	1	2	2	0	2	1	1
GRAFT OR SEW REM STS TOG.									
Pick up 1 st each side of thumb opening and k __ sts along cast on edge.	6	6	5	6	6	5	5	5	5
K across __ sts from holder.	12	10	7	10	10	7	9	7	5
K1, ssk, k __, k2tog, k to end. Work 1 rnd.	2	2	1	2	2	1	1	1	1
K1, ssk, k2tog, k to end.			*		*	*	*	*	*
K __ rnds even.	12	8	6	10	7	6	7	5	3

*Work a sl 1, k2tog, psso instead of the ssk, k2tog

What better canvas than a knitted fabric to show
off embroidery stitches? A length of yarn and a tapestry needle are all
you need to embellish an otherwise plain piece.

Popular Embroidery Stitches

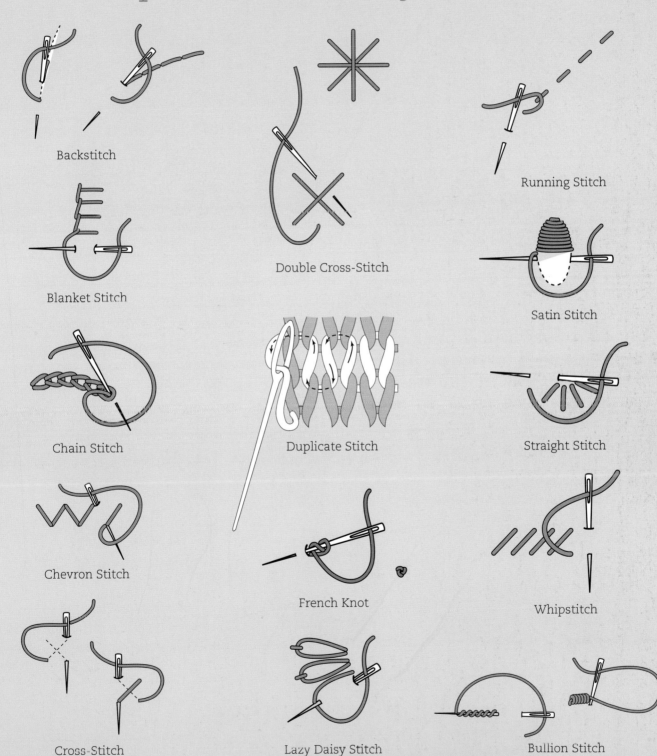

Backstitch

Running Stitch

Blanket Stitch

Double Cross-Stitch

Satin Stitch

Chain Stitch

Duplicate Stitch

Straight Stitch

Chevron Stitch

French Knot

Whipstitch

Cross-Stitch

Lazy Daisy Stitch

Bullion Stitch

a

b

Playing Footsie

c

d

Take our basic sock pattern, then leave the beaten path:
Go long or short, and embellish to your heart's content.

Designed by Charlotte Parry. Photographs by Shannon Greer

ESSENTIALS

Playing Footsie cont.

SOCKS A—POMPOM SOCKS
MATERIALS
Fortissima Socka by Schoeller+Stahl/Skacel
Collection, 1¾oz/50g balls, each approx
230yd/210m (wool/polyamide)
- **2 balls in #1404 orange**
- **1 ball in #1012 pink**
- **One set (5) size 6 (4mm) double-pointed
  needles OR SIZE TO OBTAIN GAUGE**
- **Stitch marker and holder**

●●○○

SOCKS A—POMPOM SOCKS

MEASUREMENTS
- **Leg width 2¾"/7cm (unstretched), 4"/10cm (stretched)**
- **Foot length, heel to toe 9"/23cm, or desired length**

GAUGE
22 sts and 30 rnds to 4"/10cm over St st using size 6
(4mm) dpns with 2 strands held together throughout.
TAKE TIME TO CHECK YOUR GAUGE.

NOTE
Follow instructions for basic socks on pages 44–45, with
the variations below. The basic socks were worked with
one strand of a heavier yarn. The pompom socks are
worked with 2 strands of a thin yarn held together.

POMPOM SOCKS
Cast on with double strand of orange and work in k1, p1
rib for 6"/15.5cm. Cont as for basic sock, working heel
and toe with 2 strands of red.

FINISHING
Make six 1"/2.5cm pompoms in orange and six using
orange and pink together. Sew pompoms around top
edge of cuff, alternating colors. ✪

SOCKS B—BICOLOR SOCKS
MATERIALS
Fortissima Socka by Schoeller+Stahl/Skacel
Collection, 1¾oz/50g balls, each approx
230yd/210m (wool/polyamide)
- **2 balls in #1006 green**
- **1 ball in #1005 blue**
- **One set (5) size 6 (4mm) double-pointed
  needles OR SIZE TO OBTAIN GAUGE**
- **Stitch marker and holder**

●●○○

SOCKS B—BICOLOR SOCKS

MEASUREMENTS
- **Leg width 2¾"/7cm (unstretched), 4"/10cm (stretched)**
- **Foot length, heel to toe 9"/23cm, or desired length**

GAUGE
22 sts and 30 rnds to 4"/10cm over St st using size 6
(4mm) dpns with 2 strands held together throughout.
TAKE TIME TO CHECK YOUR GAUGE.

NOTE
Follow instructions for basic socks on pages 44–45, with
the variations below. The basic socks were worked
with one strand of a heavier yarn. The bicolor socks are
worked with 2 strands of a thin yarn held together.

BICOLOR SOCKS
Cast on with double strand of green and work in k1, p1
rib for 3"/7.5cm. Cont as for basic sock, working heel
and toe with 2 strands of blue. ✪

SOCKS C—SHORT SOCKS

MATERIALS

Fortissima Socka by Schoeller+Stahl/Skacel
Collection, 1¾oz/50g balls, each approx
230yd/210m (wool/polyamide)

- 2 balls in #1010 red
- One set (5) size 6 (4mm) double-pointed
  needles OR SIZE TO OBTAIN GAUGE
- Stitch marker and holder

●●○○

SOCKS C—SHORT SOCKS

MEASUREMENTS

- Leg width 2¾"/7cm (unstretched), 4"/10cm (stretched)
- Foot length, heel to toe 9"/23cm, or desired length

GAUGE

22 sts and 30 rnds to 4"/10cm over St st using size 6
(4mm) dpns with 2 strands held together throughout.
TAKE TIME TO CHECK YOUR GAUGE.

NOTE

Follow instructions for basic socks on pages 44–45, with
the variations below. The basic socks were worked with
one strand of a heavier yarn. The short socks are worked
with 2 strands of a thin yarn held together.

SHORT SOCKS

Cast on with double strand of red and work in k1, p1 rib
for 1"/2.5cm. Cont as for basic sock. ✪

SOCKS D—STRIPED SOCKS

MATERIALS

Fortissima Socka by Schoeller+Stahl/Skacel
Collection, 1¾oz/50g balls, each approx
230yd/210m (wool/polyamide)

- 2 balls each in #1014 purple and #1017
  purple multi
- One set (5) size 6 (4mm) double-pointed
  needles OR SIZE TO OBTAIN GAUGE
- Stitch marker and holder

●●○○

SOCKS D—STRIPED SOCKS

MEASUREMENTS

- Leg width 2¾"/7cm (unstretched), 4"/10cm (stretched)
- Foot length, heel to toe 9"/23cm, or desired length

GAUGE

22 sts and 30 rnds to 4"/10cm over St st using size 6
(4mm) dpns with 2 strands held together throughout.
TAKE TIME TO CHECK YOUR GAUGE.

NOTE

Follow instructions for basic socks on pages 44–45, with
the variations below. The basic socks were worked
with one strand of a heavier yarn. The striped socks are
worked with 2 strands of a thin yarn held together.

STRIPE PATTERN

*3 rnds purple, 3 rnds multi; rep from * for stripe pat.

STRIPED SOCKS

Cast on with double strand of purple. Work in k1, p1 rib
and stripe pat for 5"/12.5cm. Work heel with 2 strands
of multi only. Cont as for basic sock, working in stripe
pat to end. ✪

ESSENTIALS

Knitting a sock is not as challenging as you might think. Here's the lowdown pages 40 and 41 were knit with double strands of yarn. For demonstration

Step-by-step

cuff

Loosely cast on 44 sts. Divide sts evenly over 4 needles—11 sts each needle. Join, taking care not to twist sts on needles. Mark end of rnd and sl marker every rnd. Work in k1, p1 rib for 3"/7.5cm. K 3 rnds.
HEEL:
K11 from first needle, then sl 11 sts from 4th needle onto other end of first needle—22 sts for heel. Sl remaining 22 sts to holder for instep. Work on heel sts as foll:
Row 1 (WS) *Sl 1, p1; rep from * to end.
Row 2 Sl 1, k to end. Rep last 2 rows 11 times more. Piece should measure approx 2½"/6.5cm.

turn heel

(Worked in short rows)
Row 1 (WS) Sl 1, p13, p2tog, leave remaining sts unworked, turn.
Row 2 Sl 1, k6, SKP, leave remaining sts unworked, turn.
Row 3 Sl 1, p6, p2tog, leave remaining sts unworked, turn. rep rows 2 and 3 until 8 sts remain.

cuff

turn heel

Kitchener stitch

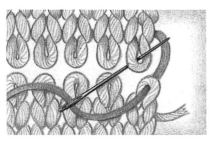

1. Insert the yarn needle purlwise into the first stitch on the front piece, then knitwise into the first stitch on the back piece. Draw the yarn through.

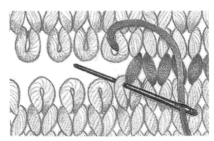

2. Insert the yarn needle knitwise into the first stitch on the front piece again. Draw the yarn through.

on how to complete a successful stocking. The colorful examples shown on purposes, we show you the basics here with a one-stranded, one-color version.

heel flap

Next rnd (RS) Using needle 1, pick up and k 12 sts along left side of heel, with another needle, k first 11 sts of instep from holder—needle 2, with another needle, k last 11 sts of instep from holder—needle 3, with another needle, pick up and k 12 sts along right side of heel, then k 4 sts from needle 1—needle 4. Needle 1 now has 16 sts, needles 2 and 3 have 11 sts each and needle 4 has 16 sts, for a total of 54 sts. Mark center of heel for end of rnd.

heel flap

instep shaping

Rnd 1 Knit.
Row 2 Needle 1: K to last 3 sts, k2tog, k1; needles 2 and 3: knit; needle 4: k1, SKP, k to end. Rep last 2 rnds 4 times more—44 sts. Work even until foot measures 8"/20.5cm from back of heel or 1¾"/4.5cm less than desired length from back of heel to end of toe.
TOE SHAPING:
Rnd 1 Needle 1: k to last 3 sts, k2tog, k1; needle 2: k1, SKP, k to end; needle 3: k to last 3 sts, k2tog, k1; needle 4: k1, SKP, k to end.
Rnd 2 Knit. Rep last 2 rnds 4 times more—24 sts. Divide sts evenly onto 2 needles and weave toe sts tog using Kitchener st (see instructions below).

instep shaping

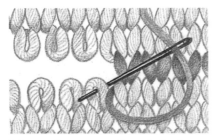

3. Insert the yarn needle purlwise into the next stitch on the front piece. Draw the yarn through.

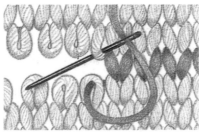

4. Insert the yarn needle purlwise into the first stitch on the back piece again. Draw the yarn through.

5. Insert the yarn needle knitwise into the next stitch on the back piece. Draw the yarn through. Repeat steps 2 through 5.

New to sock knitting? This basic pattern—perfect for first-time sock knitters—is worked in a k2, p2 rib from cuff to toe.

Ribbed Socks

MATERIALS

Happy Feet by Plymouth Yarn Company, 1¾oz/50g hanks, each approx 192yd/176m (superwash wool/nylon)

- 2 (2, 3) hanks in #12 harvest mix
- One set (5) size 1 (2.5mm) double-pointed needles (dpns) OR SIZE TO OBTAIN GAUGE
- Stitch marker
- Scrap thread (to hold sts when grafting toe)
- Tapestry needle

●●○○

Designed by Debbie O'Neill
Photographs by Paul Amato
Still-life photographs by Marcus Tullis

Sized for Child's, Woman's, Man's.

MEASUREMENTS

- **Foot circumference** 7 (8½, 9)"/18 (21.5, 23)cm
- **Foot length** 8 (10, 11)"/20.5 (25.5, 28)cm
- **Sock height** 8½ (9½, 12)"/21.5 (24, 30.5)cm

GAUGE

32 sts and 40 rnds to 4"/10cm over St st using size 1 (2.5mm) needles. TAKE TIME TO CHECK YOUR GAUGE.

K2, P2 RIB (multiple of 4 sts)

Rnd 1 *K2, p2; rep from * around.
Rep rnd 1 for k2, p2, rib.

CUFF

With size 1 (2.5mm) dpns, cast on 56 (68, 72) sts evenly divided over 4 needles, place marker (pm) and join, being careful not to twist. Work in k2, p2 rib for 6½ (7½, 9¼)"/16.5 (19, 23.5)cm.

Beg heel flap

Note Heel flap is worked back and forth on one needle over half of the sts, rem sts are on hold.

Next row With free dpn, work 14 (17, 18) sts from first needle, turn.
Next row Purl 28 (34, 36), turn.
Row 1 (RS) [Sl 1, k1] 14 (17, 18) times.
Row 2 Sl 1, p27 (33, 35).
Rep rows 1 and 2 until heel flap measures 2 (2, 2¾)"/5 (5, 7)cm.

Turn heel

Row 1 (RS) Sl 1, k15 (18, 19), SKP, k1, turn.
Row 2 Sl 1, p5, p2tog, p1, turn.
Row 3 Sl 1, k to 1 st before gap (created by turn in previous row), SKP, k1, turn.
Row 4 Sl 1, p to 1 st before gap, p2tog, p1, turn. Rep rows 3 and 4 for 3 (5, 5) times more—all heel sts have been worked.
Next row Sl 1, p to last 2 sts, p2tog.
Next row Sl 1, k to last 2 sts, SKP.
Next row (RS) Knit across 16 (18, 20) heel sts.

Gusset

Next rnd With free dpn, pick up and k 1 st in each slipped st along side edge of heel flap; [with free dpn cont in rib pat across 14 (17, 18) sts of instep] twice, with free dpn, pick up and k same number of gusset sts along 2nd side edge of heel flap, then k first half of heel sts. Beg of rnd remains the center of heel.

Ribbed Socks cont.

Next rnd With free dpn, k 2nd half of heel sts and k gusset sts (dpn #1), work first half of instep (dpn #2), work 2nd half of instep (dpn #3), k gusset sts and rem heel sts (dpn #4).
Dec rnd K to last 3 sts on dpn #1, k2tog, k1, work across instep sts on dpns #2 and #3, on dpn #4, k1, SKP, k to end of rnd.
Next rnd Work even.
Rep last 2 rnds until 56 (68, 72) sts rem. Work even until foot of sock measures 6½ (8, 9½)/16.5 (20.5, 24)cm or 1½ (2, 2½)"/4 (5, 6.5)cm shorter than desired length from heel to toe. K 1 rnd.

Toe
Dec rnd K to last 3 sts on dpn #1, k2tog, k1; on dpn #2 k1, SKP, k to end of needle; on dpn #3 k to last 3 sts, k2tog, k1; on dpn #4, k1, SKP, k to end of rnd.
Next rnd Knit.
Rep last 2 rnds until 24 sts rem. Graft toe. ⊗

Helpful Hint

• Yarns combining wool and manmade fibers are the best choice for durable knitted socks.

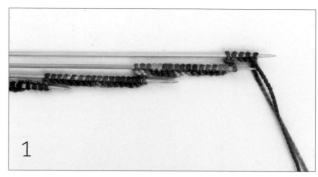

1. To cast on with double-pointed needles, using your usual method (long-tail shown), cast on sts to first needle. Hold next needle parallel and continue to cast on as usual.

2. Reposition the needles as shown, lining up the sts so they do not twist; place marker through a st on first dpn. Bring last st up to first st and knit first st to join into a round.

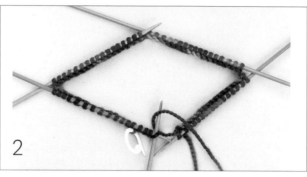

3. When the leg of the sock is the desired length, the sts for the heel flap are worked onto one needle. The instep sts remain on hold as the flap is worked back and forth, as shown.

4. The heel is turned using short rows. Work as instructed past the center of the heel, decrease, k or p1 and turn the work. A gap is formed by turning; on the next short row, the decrease closes this gap.

5. The sts for the gusset are picked up and knit along the sides of the heel flap. Insert the dpn through the edge st; wrap yarn around the needle as if to knit and draw the loop through.

6. The sts have been picked up for the gusset, and the heel has been worked onto two needles again. The marker in the sts marks the first needle; the first st on this needle is the beginning of the round.

7. When the sock is almost finished and the decreases are complete, the toe is grafted closed. With a tapestry needle and two short lengths of thread, place the top sts on one thread and the sole sts on the second and remove the dpns.

8. Cut working yarn, leaving a long tail. Thread tapestry needle and graft using duplicate stitch, working through two sts on the lower thread (photo 7) and two sts on the top thread, as shown.

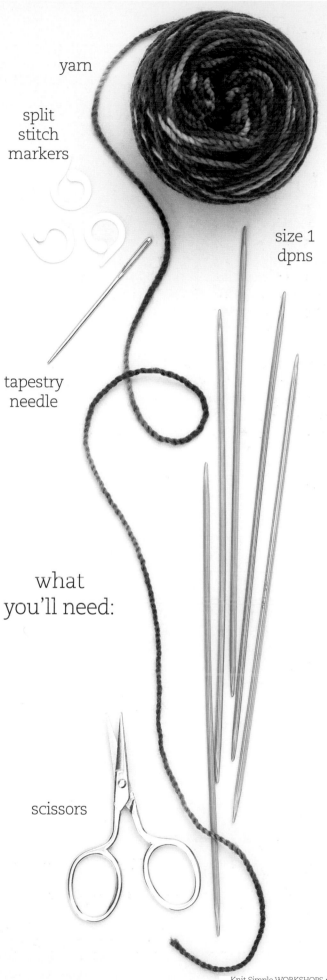

yarn

split stitch markers

size 1 dpns

tapestry needle

what you'll need:

scissors

Experiment with different decreases as you make headway on a simple head covering perfect for a breezy day.

Head Scarf

MATERIALS

Sonata by The Great Adirondack Yarn Co., 3oz/85g skeins, each approx 200yd/183m (nylon)

- **1 skein in irish cream**
- **One size 7 (4.5mm) circular needle, 29"/74cm long OR SIZE TO OBTAIN GAUGE**
- **Two pairs of size 7 (4.5mm) double-pointed needles (dpns) for ties**

●○○○

Designed by Linda Cyr
Photographs by Marcus Tullis

MEASUREMENTS

Approx 18"/45.5cm wide x 13"/33cm at longest point (without ties)

GAUGE

20 sts and 28 rows to 4"/10cm over St st using size 7 (4.5mm) needles. TAKE TIME TO CHECK YOUR GAUGE.

Note A circular needle is used to accommodate the large number of sts. Work back and forth in rows.

HEAD SCARF

Cast on 91 sts. **Row 1 (RS)** SSK, k to last 2 sts, k2tog. **Row 2** Purl. Rep rows 1 and 2 until 3 sts rem, ending with a WS row.
Next row Sl 1, k2tog, psso. Fasten off.

TIES (make 2) With dpn, cast on 4 sts. Work I-cord as foll:

*Next row (RS) K4. Slide sts back to beg of needle so that next row is a RS row; rep from * until tie measures 10"/25.5cm long. Bind off.

FINISHING

Sew ends of ties to long edge of scarf, letting edge roll around ties. ✪

how to decrease

Knit 2 together (k2tog): Insert right-hand needle knitwise into next two stitches as shown, then knit them off the needle.

Purl 2 together (p2tog): Insert right-hand needle purlwise into the next two stitches as shown, then purl them off the needle.

Slip, slip, knit (ssk): Slip the next two stitches knitwise, one at a time, to the left-hand needle as shown.

Insert the left-hand needle into the front of these two slipped stitches as shown and knit them together.

Slip, knit 2 together, pass over (SK2P): Slip the next stitch knitwise, knit the next two stitches together, then pass the slipped stitch over the knit 2 together, as shown.

Begin this shawl with one stitch, then increase stitches on either side to create a triangle as wide as desired.

Triangular Shawl

MATERIALS

Giotto by Colinette, 3½oz/100g skeins, each approx 157yd/ 144m (cotton/rayon/nylon)

- **4 skeins in #137 banwy**
- **One size 10 (6mm) circular needle 29"/ 74cm long OR SIZE TO OBTAIN GAUGE**

●○○○

Designed by Linda Cyr
Photographs by Paul Amato

MEASUREMENTS

Approx 62"/157.5cm wide x 40"/101.5cm at longest point

GAUGE

13 sts and 20 rows to 4"/10cm over St st using size 10 (6mm) needle. TAKE TIME TO CHECK YOUR GAUGE.

Note A circular needle is used to accommodate the large number of sts. Work back and forth in rows.

SHAWL

Make a slipknot and place on needle.
Row 1 (RS) K1, yo, k1 into slipknot.
Row 2 Purl.
Row 3 K1, yo, k to last st, yo, k1. Rep rows 2 and 3 until there are 201 sts. Piece measures approx 62"/157.5cm wide and 40"/101.5cm (measured at center). Loosely bind off all sts. ▌

how to increase

Basic increase: Knit into front of stitch and, without dropping it from needle, knit into the back loop of the same stitch.

Yarn over increase: Bring the yarn from back to front to back between the two needles, then knit the next stitch.

On the following row, purl the yarn over in the usual way. This increase creates a decorative hole, or "eyelet," in the fabric.

Make one (M1) increase: Insert right-hand needle from front to back into the horizontal strand between two stitches, as shown.

Place strand on the left-hand needle, as shown, then knit it through the back loop. This increase must be worked at least one stitch in from the edge.

New to cabling? Lay the groundwork with a quick-stitching accessory.

Cabled Headband

MATERIALS

Lavish by Classic Elite Yarns, 1¾oz/50g balls, each approx 125yd/115m (cashmere)

- **1 ball in #92560 light blue**
- **Size 10 (6mm) circular needle, 16"/40.5cm, OR SIZE TO OBTAIN GAUGE**
- **Cable needle**

●●○○

Designed by Lipp Holmfeld
Photograph by Rose Callahan

FINISHED MEASUREMENTS

- 3½"/9cm wide x 22"/56cm long (can be made to any length)

GAUGES

14 sts and 28 rows to 4"/10cm over St st, using size 10 (6mm) needle.
16 sts and 20 rows to 4"/10cm over pat st, using size 10 (6mm) needle.
TAKE TIME TO CHECK YOUR GAUGES

NOTES

Front of headband can be worked on straight or circular needles.
Underside of headband is worked on circular needles.

HEADBAND

Front
Cast on 16 sts.
Row 1 (WS) P1, k1, p2, k2, p4, k2, p2, k1, p1.
Row 2 (RS) P1, k3, p2, k4, p2, k3, p1.
Row 3 and all WS rows Work as for row 1.
Row 4 P1, k3, p2, sl 2 sts to cn and hold to *front*, k2, k2 from cn, p2, k3, p1.
Row 6 P1, k1, sl 1 st to cn and hold in *back*, k1, k1 from cn, p2, k4, p2, sl 1 st to cn and hold in *back*, k1, k1 from cn, k1, pl.
Rep rows 1–6 19 times more, rep rows 1 and 2 once more. Bind off.

FINISHING

*Sew 2 short edges tog.

Underside
With RS of work facing, starting at seam, pick up and k 62 sts (approx 1 st in every other row), mark beg of rnd. K for 20 rounds. Fold piece in half along first row of underside with RS of front of headband visible. Inserting needle through next st on needle and into opposite edge of headband at same time to join the 2 long edges, bind off *loosely*. ✪

4-stitch left cable

1. To twist the stitches to the left without a cable needle, skip the first two stitches on the left-hand needle and knit the third stitch from behind, as shown here.

2. Let the two stitches drop to the front of the work, then knit the fourth stitch. The stitches at the front will not unravel. Slip the two dropped stitches back on the left-hand needle as shown, and knit them.

3. To work the cable to the right, begin by working the third stitch in front of the first two stitches, letting them fall to the back. Complete the cable as before.

The beauty of this technique—called "mosaic knitting"—is that you will never have to carry another color across the wrong side.

Mosaic Scarf

MATERIALS
Baby Twist by Alpaca With A Twist, 1¾oz/50g skeins, each approx 110yd/100m (baby alpaca)

- **2 skeins each in #1008 blue corn (MC) and #1004 cloudy sky (CC)**
- **One pair size 6 (4mm) needles OR SIZE TO OBTAIN GAUGE**

●●○○

Designed by Tanis Gray
Photograph by Rose Callahan

MEASUREMENTS
Approximately 8 x 60"/20.5 x152.5cm

GAUGE
19 sts and 32 rows to 4"/10cm over slip st pattern, using size 6 (4mm) needles.
TAKE TIME TO CHECK YOUR GAUGE.

MOSAIC PATTERN
(multiple of 12 sts plus 2)
Row 1 (RS) With MC, knit.
Row 2 With MC, purl.
Row 3 With CC, *sl 2 wyib, k10; rep from * end sl 2 wyib.
Row 4 With CC, sl 2 wyif, *k10, sl 2 wyif; rep from * to end.
Rows 5–8 Rep rows 1–4.
Rows 9 and 10 Rep rows 1 and 2.
Row 11 With CC, *k6, sl 2 wyib, k4; rep from *, end k2.
Row 12 With CC, k2, *k4, sl 2 wyif, k6; rep from * to end.
Rows 13–16 Rep rows 9–12.
Rep rows 1–16 for mosaic pattern.

SCARF
With MC and size 6 (4mm) needles, cast on 38 sts.
Beg mosaic pat
Work in slip st pat until scarf measures approx 60"/20.5cm from beg. Bind off with MC. ✪

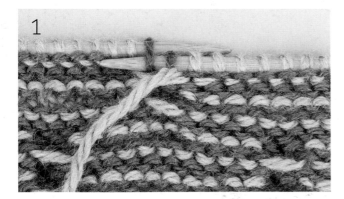

Here we show row 4 of the pattern, a wrong-side row, where you knit the pale blue stitches and slip the dark blue ones. Bring the yarn to the front of the work and slip the next two stitches purlwise.

Now bring the yarn to the back of the work, making sure that the strand goes *between* the two needles and *not over* the right needle. Don't pull too tightly or the fabric will pucker.

Bright and breezy, these picot-edged hat-and-mitten duos can be striped and embellished in your choice of colors and embroidery.

Hat and Mitten Set

MATERIALS

MinnowMerino from the Jil Eaton Collection/ Classic Elite Yarns, 1¾oz/50g skeins, each approx 77yd/70m (extrafine merino wool)
- 2 skeins in #4747 bluette (MC) or #4735 chartreuse (MC)
- 1 skein each in #4735 chartreuse (A) or #4747 bluette (A) and #4720 aqua (B)
- One set (5) size 7 (4.5mm) dpns OR SIZE TO OBTAIN GAUGE
- Stitch marker and holder

●●○○

Designed by Jil Eaton
Photographs by Rose Callahan
Still-life photographs by Marcus Tullis

Both hat and mittens are sized for Child's (Woman's).

MEASUREMENTS
- **Circumference** 17¾ (21)"/45 (53)cm

GAUGE
20 sts and 26 rnds to 4"/10cm over St st using size 7 (4.5mm) needles. TAKE TIME TO CHECK YOUR GAUGE.

TOP OF HAT
With 2 dpn and MC, cast on 4 sts. Work I-cord as foll: **Row 1 (RS)** K4. *Do not turn work. Slide sts to other end of needle to work next row from RS and k4; rep from * for 4 rows.

BODY
Next row Inc 1 st in each st—8 sts. Divide sts evenly over 4 dpn (2 sts on each needle). Join, placing marker for beg of rnd, and work in rnds of St st (k every rnd), inc 1 st at end of every needle every rnd (therefore 4 sts inc'd every rnd) until there are 88 (104) sts, or 22 (26) sts on each needle. (**Note** To make hat smaller or larger, work a multiple of 4 fewer or 4 more increases.) For turning ridge, p 4 rnds. (**Note** For green version, work the body in stripes as foll: *3 rnds MC, 2 rnds A; rep from * (5 rnds) for stripe pat.) Cont in St st with MC only or in stripe pat, for 2½(3)"/6.5 (7.5)cm, or desired depth. **Picot rnd** *K2tog, yo; rep from * around. Cont in St st with MC only for 1"/2.5cm. Bind off.
Embroidery: For striped version, work French knots with B in center of MC stripe in every 6th st and alternating placement on 2nd stripe (see photo). For solid version, make French knots with B randomly and work lazy daisy flower petals around some of the knots (see photo).

FINISHING
Fold bound-off edge to inside at picot rnd and sew in place.

MITTENS
With MC, cast on 32 (40) sts and divide evenly over 4 dpn. Work in St st for 4 rnds. **Picot rnd** *K2tog, yo; rep from * around. Cont in St st for 1½ (3)"/4 (7.5)cm. (**Note** For green version, work the cuff in stripes as foll: *3 rnds MC, 2 rnds A; rep from * (5 rnds) for stripe pat.)
Thumb gusset: Next rnd Inc 1 st in next st, k1, inc in next st, work to end. Work 2 rnds even. **Next rnd** Inc 1, k3, inc 1, work to end. Work 2 rnds even. **Next rnd** Inc 1, k5, inc 1, work to end. Work 2 rnds even. **For Woman's size only** Inc 1, k7, inc 1, work to end. Work 2 rnds even.
Thumb: For both sizes—Next rnd Working over three needles, k first 9 (11) sts for thumb, place rem 29 (37) sts on holder for hand. **Next rnd** Cast on 3 sts, k to end of rnd—12 (14) sts. Work even in St st for 1½ (2)"/

Hat and Mitten Set cont.

4 (5)cm, or desired depth. **Next rnd** [K2, k2tog] 3 times, k0 (2)—9 (11) sts. **Next rnd** [K1, k2tog] 3 times, k0 (2)—6 (8) sts. **Next rnd** K2tog around. Cut yarn and draw through rem 3 (4) sts.
Hand: Next rnd Sl 29 (37) sts from holder back to 4 needles and pick up 3 sts along cast-on thumb sts—32 (40) sts. Cont in rnds of St st for 3 (4)"/7.5 (10)cm, or desired depth.

Shape top

Next rnd *K2, k2tog; rep from * around—24 (30) sts. K 2 rnds. **Next rnd** *K1, k2tog; rep from * around—18 (20) sts. K 2 rnds. **Next rnd** *K2tog; rep from * around. K 1 rnd. Cut yarn and draw through rem 9 (10) sts.

FINISHING

Fold cast-on edge to inside at picot rnd and sew in place. Embroider as for hats. ✪

Helpful Hint

- Tag-team the mittens in a mini knitting circle: You stitch one and give the other to your tween or teen knitter. There's nothing like bonding over knitted must-haves.

from the top

Working a hat from the top down is the way to go for difficult-to-fit heads. Just work increase rows until you reach the desired size.
1. Make a 4-st I-cord using 2 dpns for top nub (see background photo).

These quick and easy combos are fun to knit in the round from the top down, leaving behind no seams and plenty of pizazz.

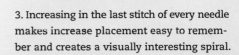

2. Divide 8 sts evenly over 4 dpns for knitting in the round.

3. Increasing in the last stitch of every needle makes increase placement easy to remember and creates a visually interesting spiral.

french knot

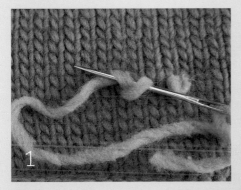

Place French knots randomly on the blue set and as part of the stripe pattern on the green set. 1. Bring yarn back to front and wrap it twice around tapestry needle, holding yarn taut.

2. Reinsert needle close to where the yarn emerged and pull the yarn through to the wrong side, holding the knot in place with your finger.

lazy daisy

Make flowers around the French knots. 1. Bring yarn up through back, close to the French knot. Reinsert needle into same place, then bring it up again from the back, about a half-inch away. Wrap the yarn around the needle to form a loop.

2. Pull yarn through. Insert needle above loop, securing it. Working the same way, make 2 or 3 more petals for flowers.

Square a square; triple a triangle: If you can pick up stitches, you can master modular knitting.

Triangle Hat and Scarf

MATERIALS

Supermerino by Artyarns, 1¾oz/50g balls, each approx 104yd/94m (superwash wool)
- 3 skeins in #135 orange multi (MC)
- 1 skein in #246 black (CC)
- One pair and one circular needle, 16"/40cm long, each size 7 (4.5mm) OR SIZE TO OBTAIN GAUGE
- Stitch holder and marker

●●○○

Designed by Iris Schreier
Photographs by Paul Amato

MEASUREMENTS

Scarf 2½" x 34"/6.5cm x 86.5cm
Hat Circumference 20"/51cm

GAUGE

32 sts and 24 rows to 4"/10cm over k1, p1 rib (unstretched).
TAKE TIME TO CHECK YOUR GAUGE.

SCARF (make 2 pieces)

With straight needles and CC, cast on 50 sts. Work in St st for 4 rows. Cut CC, join MC, leaving a 10"/25.5cm tail (used for closing hole later). Cont with MC as foll:

TRIANGLE 1

Row 1 K in front and back of next st (inc 1), turn; sl 1, turn—1 st left unknitted. **Row 2** Inc 1, k1, turn; sl 1, k1, turn—2 sts left unknitted. **Row 3** Inc 1, k2, turn; sl 1, k2, turn—3 sts left unknitted. **Row 4** Inc 1, k3, turn; sl 1, k3, turn—4 sts left unknitted. **Row 5** Inc 1, k4, turn; sl 1, k4, turn—5 sts left unknitted. **Row 6** Inc 1, k5, turn; sl 1, k5, turn—6 sts left unknitted. **Row 7** Inc 1, k6, turn; sl 1, k6, turn—7 sts left unknitted. **Row 8** Inc 1, k7, turn; sl 1, k7, turn—8 sts left unknitted. **Row 9** Inc 1, k8, turn; sl 1, k8, turn—9 sts left unknitted. **Row 10** Inc 1, k9, do not turn.

TRIANGLE 2

Row 1 K1, turn; ssk, turn. **Row 2** Sl 1, k1, turn; sl 1, ssk, turn. **Row 3** Sl 1, k2, turn; sl 1, k1, ssk, turn. **Row 4** Sl 1, k3, turn; sl 1, k2, ssk, turn. **Row 5** Sl 1, k4, turn; sl 1, k3, ssk, turn. **Row 6** Sl 1, k5, turn; sl 1, k4, ssk, turn. **Row 7** Sl 1, k6, turn; sl 1, k5, ssk, turn. **Row 8** Sl 1, k7, turn; sl 1, k6, ssk, turn. **Row 9** Sl 1, k8, turn; sl 1, k7, ssk, turn. **Row 10** Sl 1, k9, turn; sl 1, k8, ssk, turn. **Row 11** Sl 1, k9, do not turn. Rep rows 1–11 of Triangle 2 three more times. There will be a total of 5 triangles—21 sts on needle. Work in k1, p1 rib with MC until piece measures 17"/43cm from beg. Place sts on holder. Work a second piece in the same way.

FINISHING

Join both pieces tog using 3-needle bind off as foll: Hold right sizes of pieces tog on two needles, insert third needle knitwise into first st on each needle and k these 2 sts tog, *p next st on both needles tog as before. Slip the first st on the 3rd needle over the 2nd st and off the needle. Rep from * (alternating k2tog and p2tog) until all sts are bound off. Thread tapestry needle with tail, and weave yarn in and out of tops of 5 triangles; tighten to close center hole. Make a knot to fasten. Weave in all ends.

HAT

With circular needle and CC, cast on 84 sts for brim. Join, placing marker for end of rnd, taking care not to twist sts on needles. Work in

Triangle hat and scarf cont.

St st (k every rnd) for 4 rnds. Cut CC, join MC work in garter st (k 1 rnd, p 1 rnd) for 3"/7.5cm, or desired hat brim height.

CROWN

Note There are 14 sts in each of the 6 triangles that create the crown of the hat.

TRIANGLE 1

Rows 1–9 Rep rows 1–9 of triangle 1 in scarf. **Row 10** Inc 1, k9; turn; sl 1, k9, turn—10 sts left unknitted **Row 11** Inc 1, k10, turn; sl 1, k10, turn—11 sts left unknitted **Row 12** Inc 1, k11, turn; sl 1, k11, turn—12 sts left unknitted **Row 13** Inc 1, k12, turn, sl 1, k12, turn—13 sts left unknitted **Row 14** Inc 1, k13, do *not* turn. Slip 14 sts from right to left side of the circular needle. Place the 13 sts that have been left unknitted and the first st of the Inc 1 in row 14 on st holder. These 14 sts will be used at the end of the project to attach the 6th triangle. Slip 14 sts back to right side of the circular needle.

TRIANGLE 2

Rows 1–10 Rep rows 1–10 of triangle 2 in Scarf. **Row 11** Sl 1, k10, turn; sl 1, k9, ssk, turn. **Row 12** Sl 1, k11, turn; sl 1, k10, ssk, turn. **Row 13** Sl 1, k12, turn; sl 1, k11, ssk, turn. **Row 14** Sl 1, k13, turn; sl 1, k12, ssk, turn. **Row 15** Sl 1, k13.
Rep rows 1–15 of triangle 2 four more times—6 triangles.

FINISHING

Turn hat inside out. Join 14 sts on stitch holder 1 with 14 sts left from 6th triangle as foll: Move sts from st holder to an extra needle, facing them in the same direction as the sts from triangle 6. Use the 3-needle bind-off method as in scarf to join the sts. Cut yarn, leaving approx a 5"/12.5cm tail. Thread tapestry needle with tail, and weave yarn in and out through all the topmost triangle sts to close hole at top. Pull tightly, knot and weave in any ends. ✿

Helpful Hints

- For garter-stitch pieces, place a safety pin on the front side of the work to keep track of your rows.
- When working the center decreases, pull the yarn tightly to prevent holes.
- If substituting yarn, make one motif and measure across the widest point to determine the finished size.
- If you have lots of disparate colors you'd like to use up, separate them with strips of black.

three needle bind-off

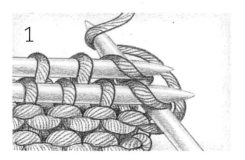

With the right side of the two pieces facing each other and the needles parallel, insert a third needle knitwise into the first stitch of each needle. Wrap the yarn around the needle as if to knit.

Knit these two stitches together and slip them off the needles. *Knit the next two stitches together in the same way as shown.

Slip the first stitch on the third needle over the second stitch and off the needle. Repeat from the * in step 2 across the row until all the stitches are bound off.

modular workshop

To create the six triangles at the top of the hat, work each section back and forth in garter stitch. We have used a length of yarn to hold the 14 stitches at the side of the first triangle.

Join the open stitches of ribbing at the center of the scarf using the three-needle bind-off method. The above photo shows you how to purl the stitch on the back needle together with the stitch on the front needle.

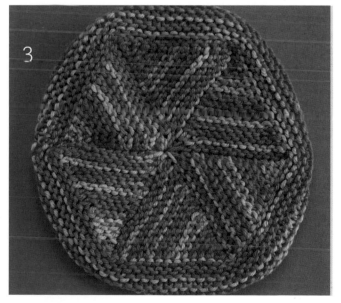

The finished hat as seen from the top.

ACCESSORIES

Craft imitates nature: Six petals curl around a center bud.
Delicate leaves add a breath of spring.

Bouquet of Crochet

MATERIALS

• DMC Six-Strand Embroidery Floss, each skein 8.7yd/8m (100% cotton)

For each flower:

1 skein in each of two colors (choose from #601 dark cranberry, #602 medium cranberry, #606 bright orange-red, #666 light christmas red, #818 baby pink, #891 dark carnation, #947 burnt orange, #963 ultimate very light dusty rose, #3801 christmas red, #B5200 bright white) or colors of your choice

For each leaf:

1 skein of green (choose from #164 light green, #472 avocado green ultimate light, #703 chartreuse and #912 light emerald green) or colors of your choice

• Steel crochet hooks #0 (3.25mm) for flower and size 2 (2.25mm) for leaves

Photograph by Rose Callahan

SIZES

Small (Medium, Large) flowers

MEASUREMENTS

Flower circumference 1½ (2, 2½)"/4 (5, 6.5)cm

GAUGE

6 sc = 1"/2.5cm with #0 (3.25mm) hook

FLOWER CENTER

With first flower color, ch 9 (13, 17). **Row 1:** Work 2 sc in 2nd ch from hook and in each ch to end—16 (24, 32) sc. Ch 1, turn. **Row 2:** Work 2 sc in each sc—32 (48, 64) sc. Ch 1, turn. **Next 1 (2, 3) rows:** Work sc in each sc, working ch 1 to turn at end of each row. Fasten off.

INNER PETALS (make 3)

With 2nd flower color, ch 4 (5, 7). **Row 1:** Work 2 sc in 2nd ch from hook and in each ch to end—6 (8, 12) sc. Ch 1, turn. **Row 2:** Work 2 sc in each sc—12 (16, 24) sc. Ch 1, turn. Work 0 (1, 3) rows even in sc. **Next 2 rows:** Sc2tog each side of every row—8 (12, 20)sts. Work 1 row even in sc. Fasten off.

OUTER PETALS (make 3)

With 2nd flower color, ch 5 (6, 8). **Row 1:** Work 2 sc in 2nd ch from hook and in each ch to end—4 (5, 7) sc. Ch 1, turn. **Row 2:** Work 2 sc in each sc—16 (20, 28) sc. Ch 1, turn. Work 0 (1, 3) rows even in sc. **Next 3 rows:** Dec 1 st each side of every row—10 (14, 22) sts. Work 1 row even in sc. Fasten off.

LEAVES (make 3)

With a leaf color, ch 11 (15, 19). **Rnd 1:** Work sc in 2nd ch from hook, work tr in next 2 ch, work dc in next 4 (8, 12) ch, work 2 tr in next 2 ch, work sc in last ch; work in same way along opposite edge of foundation chain, join with sl st to first st. For Small flower only: Fasten off. **Next rnd—for Medium and Large flower only:** Work 1 sc in each st, working 3 sc at point of leaf, join to first sc. Fasten off.

FINISHING

Weave in all ends. Roll the center piece around itself and tack closed at several points. Wrap the inner petals around the center and sew in place at the base. Attach the outer petals in same way. Pin the leaves to the flower as desired, then sew them in place. ✪

Shown here is a completed treble from Rnd 1 on the leaf.

Roll the 3 sc strips around each other to form the flower.

On the wrong side, pin the leaves, then sew in place.

To make a brooch, stitch a pin back to the back of the flower.

Vertical bands of color are worked singularly and hooked together; there are no errant ends to work in.

Hairpin Lace

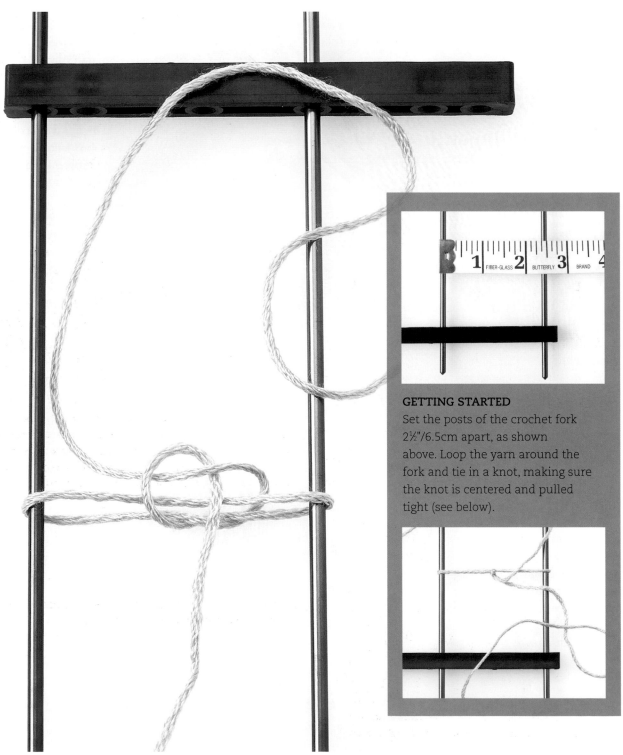

GETTING STARTED
Set the posts of the crochet fork 2½"/6.5cm apart, as shown above. Loop the yarn around the fork and tie in a knot, making sure the knot is centered and pulled tight (see below).

All you need to know about hairpin lace

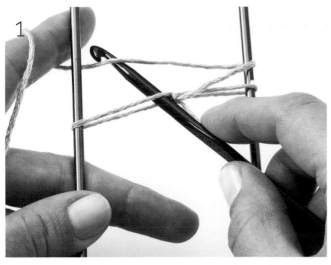

1

With working yarn wrapped around fork from front to back, put the crochet hook into the middle of the loop next to the knot, as shown, and draw a loop through.

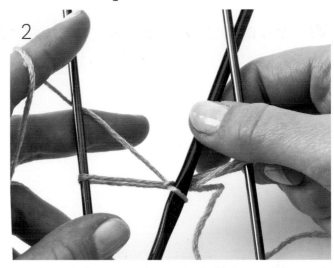

2

Move the end of the crochet hook to back of fork. Turn fork toward you so that working yarn wraps from front to back. The right side of fork will now be the left side.

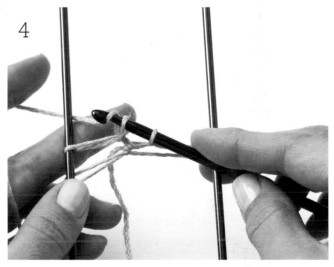

3

Move crochet hook between the two completed loops and draw the yarn through—2 loops on hook.

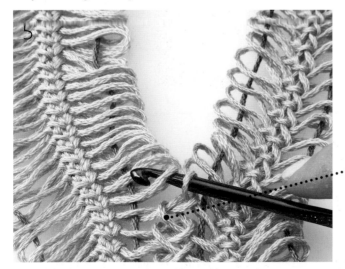

4

Draw yarn through 2 loops on hook to complete the single crochet. Repeat steps 2–4 for hairpin lace. To join completed strips (see bottom left), pull loop from one side through corresponding loop on the other, as shown. Work your way up, alternating sides. Hold last loop in place with a safety pin until you add fringe.

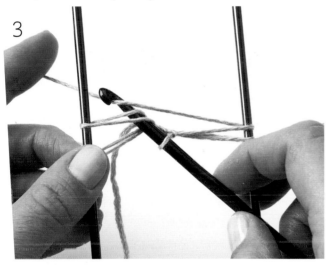

5

Half a dozen shades of Caron's "Country" are made in separate strips using a hairpin-lace fork from Boye (www.wrights.com).

Vertical bands of color are worked singularly and hooked together; there are no errant ends to weave in.

Taking I-cord from afterthought to star attraction is a breeze,
once you know the ropes.

I-Cord Magic

Photographs by David Lazarus and Marcus Tullis

knitting I-cord with two dpns

To knit I-cord, you'll need two double-pointed needles or one circular needle. For the cord shown, cast on 4 sts. 1) Knit one row. Do not turn.
2) Slide stitches to other end of needle to work the next row from the right side. Bringing yarn across back of work, k4. Repeat Steps 1 and 2.

Knitting-Nancy know-how

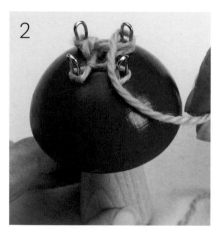

Thread end of yarn through hole, from top to bottom, leaving a 4"/10cm tail, and secure with left hand. Wrap the yarn from the ball counterclockwise around each of the four pegs, as shown.

Working in a clockwise direction, wrap the yarn counterclockwise once more around all four pegs, as shown. You are now ready to knit off the loops.

Using the provided stylus or hook, lift the bottom loop over the top loop and off the first peg. Repeat Step 3 around all pegs. Repeat Steps 2 and 3 to desired length.

Lion Brand Spool Knitter; lionbrand.com

Bond America Embellish-Knit!;
bond-america.com

Pony French Knitter; ponyneedles.com

Boye Knit Spool from Wrights;
wrights.com/wrights

Skacel Collection Addi Turbo double-pointed
needles; www.skacelknitting.com

Haba Knitting Mushroom;
usillygoose.com/knmu.html

Susan Bates Knitting Knobby;
www.coatsandclark.com/products/accessories

Skacel Collection hardwood Knitting Spool;
www.skacelknitting.com

Bates Crystalites French Knitter;
www.coatsandclark.com/products/accessories

Knit her a bag she'll love! Then tie pompoms to the ends of the drawstrings and she's set for a shopping expedition.

Drawstring Bag With Pompoms

MATERIALS

Classic Wool by Patons, 3½oz/100g skeins, each approx 223yd/205m (wool)

- 1 skein each in #202 aran (MC), #77732 that's pink (A), #77734 too teal (B), #218 peacock (C) and #212 royal purple (D)
- One pair size 7 (4.5mm) needles OR SIZE TO OBTAIN GAUGE
- Two size 7 (4.5mm) double-pointed needles (dpns) for I-cord
- Size G/6 (4mm) crochet hook
- One pair 5"/12.5cm diameter round clear plastic purse handles

●●○○

Designed by Jeannie Chin
Photographs by Rose Callahan

MEASUREMENTS

9" x 7"/23cm x 17.5cm (excluding handles)

GAUGE

22 sts and 29 rows to 4"/10cm over St st using size 7 (4.5mm) needles. TAKE TIME TO CHECK YOUR GAUGE

BACK

With MC, cast on 68 sts.

Row 1 (RS) P1, k2, *p2, k2; rep from *, end p1.

Row 2 K1, p2, [k2, p2]; rep from *, end k1. Rep rows 1 and 2 until piece measures 4"/10cm from beg, end with a WS row. Bind off 5 sts at beg of next 2 rows—58 sts. Cont in rib pat as established until piece measures 5½"/14cm from beg, end with a WS row.

Next (eyelet) row (RS) K2, *yo, p2tog, k2; rep from * to end—14 eyelets.

Next row P2, *k2, p2; rep from * to end. Cont in rib pat as established until piece measures 8¼"/21cm from beg, end with a WS row. Bind off in rib.

FRONT

Work as for back.

BOTTOM GUSSET

With MC, cast on 50 sts. Work even in St st for 1½"/4cm. Bind off.

FINISHING

Sew side seams of front and back tog. Pin bottom gusset to bottom opening of bag, making sure to center side seams on short side edges of gusset. Sew in place.

Handles (make 2)

With crochet hook and A, make a slipknot, leaving a 4"/10cm tail, then place slipknot on crochet hook.

Rnd 1 (RS) Join A to a handle with a sc. Making sure to work fairly tightly and evenly, work sc over handle until completely covered, join rnd with a sl st in first st. Fasten off. Fold top edge of front over to WS around handle, so bound-off edge is 2 rows above eyelet row; sew edge in place. Rep for back.

Flowers (make 3)

With crochet hook and B, ch 5, leaving a long tail for sewing. Join ch with sl st forming a ring. **Rnd 1 (RS)** [Ch 3, 2 dc, ch 3, sl st] 5 times in ring. Fasten off leaving long tail for sewing. Pull beg tail on WS to draw petals tog; make a few stitches to secure. Make one more flower each using B and C. Using A, make 3 French knots in center of each flower.

Leaves (make 3)

With crochet hook and D, ch 7.

Row 1 (RS) Working in back lps of ch, sl st in 2nd ch from hook, sc in next ch, hdc in next ch, dc in next 2 ch, ch 2, sl st in last ch, ch 2; turn to work in rem front lps of ch, work as foll: dc in first 2 ch, 1 hdc in

Lesson of the day: Kid-happy hues + funky zippers + easy stitching = "Can I wear it again tomorrow?"

Multi-Zipper Cardigan

Sized for Child's 4, 6, 8, 10. Shown in size 4.

MATERIALS

Creative Focus Superwash by Nashua Handknits/Westminster Fibers, 3½oz/ 100g skeins, each approx 218yd/199m (merino blended superwash wool)

- 3 (4, 5, 5) skeins in #15 lilac (MC)
- 1 skein in #6 pale green (CC)
- One pair each sizes 6 and 8 (4 and 5mm) needles OR SIZE TO OBTAIN GAUGE
- One separating zipper, 14 (16, 18, 18)"/30 (35, 40, 45, 45)cm, from Coats & Clark, F23 Style, #256 natural
- 4 all-purpose zippers, 4"/10cm, from Coats & Clark, F72 style, 2 each in #4 blue and #30 light pink
- Sewing needle, thread and straight pins

●●●○

Designed by Victoria Hilditch
Photographs by Rose Callahan

MEASUREMENTS

- **Chest (closed)** 29 (31, 33, 35)"/73.5 (78.5, 84, 89)cm
- **Length** 15 (17, 19, 20)"/38 (43, 48, 51)cm
- **Upper arm** 9½ (10, 11, 11½)"/24 (25.5, 28, 29)cm

GAUGE

18 sts and 24 rows to 4"/10cm over St st using larger needles.
TAKE TIME TO CHECK YOUR GAUGE.

K1, P1, RIB (over an odd number of sts)

Row 1 *K1, p1; rep from *, end k1.
Row 2 K the knit sts, and p the purl sts.
Rep row 2 for k1, p1 rib.

BACK

With smaller needles and MC, cast on 65 (69, 73, 77) sts. Work in k1, p1 rib for 2"/5cm, dec 1 (1, 1, 0) st on last row—64 (68, 72, 77) sts. Change to larger needles and work in St st (k on RS, p on WS) until piece measures 9½ (11, 12½, 13)"/24 (28, 31.5, 33)cm from beg.

Shape armhole

Bind off 3 (4, 4, 5) sts at beg of next 2 rows, 2 (2, 3, 3) sts at beg of next 2 rows, dec 1 st each side every other row 4 (4, 4, 5) times—46 (48, 50, 51) sts. Work even until armhole measures 5½ (6, 6½, 7)"/14 (15, 16.5, 17.5)cm. Bind off all sts.

LEFT FRONT

With smaller needles and MC, cast on 33 (35, 37, 39) sts. Work in k1, p1 rib for 2"/5cm, dec 1 st on last row—32 (34, 36, 38) sts. Change to larger needles and work in St st until piece measures 4 (4½, 5, 5)"/10 (11.5, 12.5, 12.5)cm from beg, end with a WS row.

Zipper opening row (RS) K5 (6, 8, 9), bring yarn to front, slip next st purlwise. Place yarn at back and leave it there.
*Slip next st from LH needle, pass the first slipped st over it; rep from * 17 times more (not moving the yarn).
Slip the last bound-off st to LH needle and turn work. Cast on 19 sts (using the cable cast-on method) as foll: *with yarn at back of work, insert RH needle between the first and 2nd sts on LH needle draw up a loop, place the loop on LH needle; rep from * 18 times more, turn work. Sl first st with yarn at back from LH needle and pass extra cast-on st over it, k to end of row. Cont in St st until piece measures 8 (9, 10, 10½)"/20.5 (23, 25.5, 26.5)cm from beg, end with a WS row. Work zipper opening row. Cont in St st until piece measures 9½ (11, 12½, 13)"/24 (28, 31.5, 33)cm from beg. Shape armhole at side edge as for back on RS rows—23 (24, 25, 25) sts. Work even until armhole measures 3½ (4, 4½, 4)"/9 (10, 11.5, 10)cm, end with a RS row.

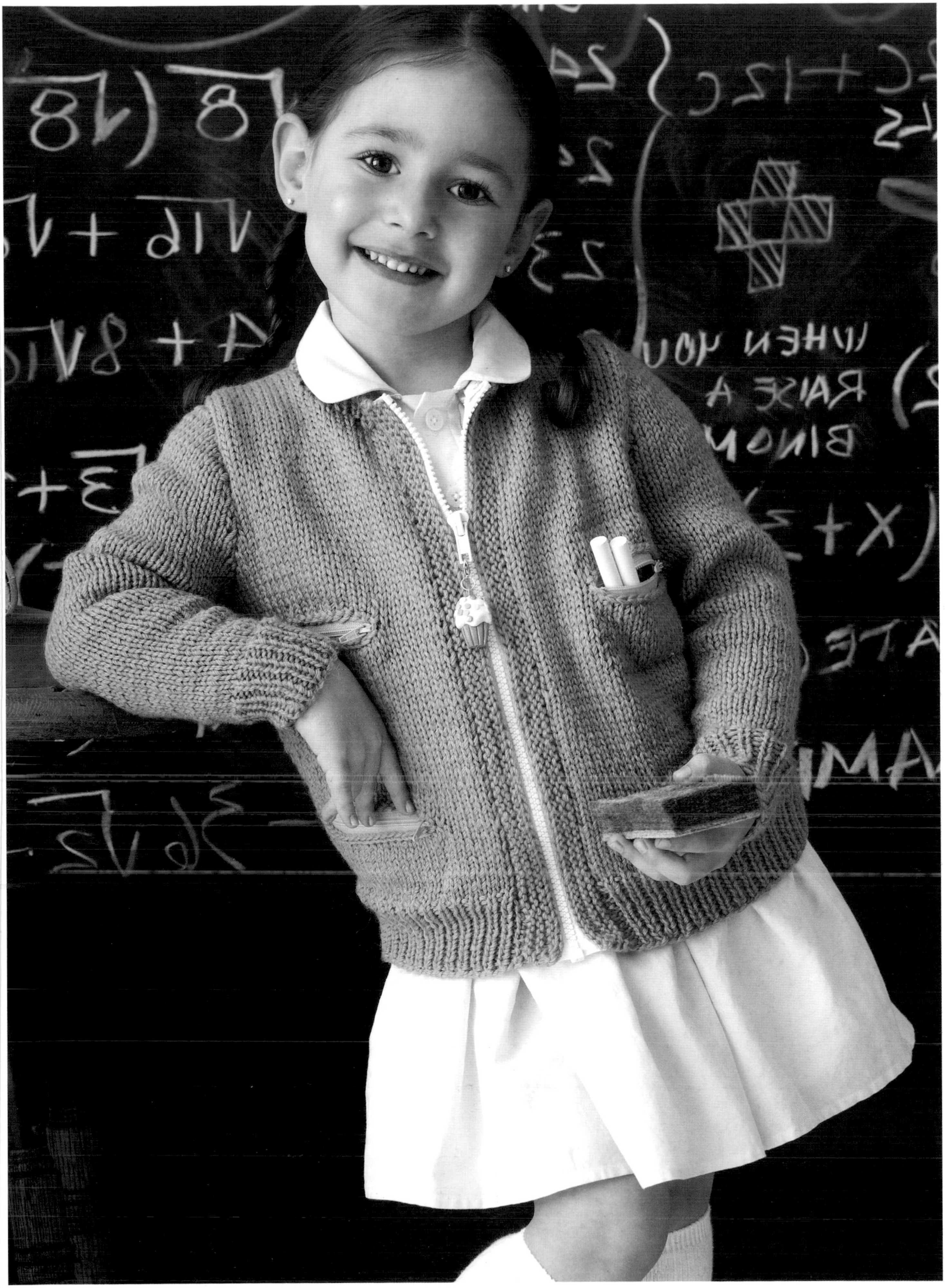

EASY TOPS

Add a new technique to your repertoire: knitting in one piece from the top down. Not only does this technique let you easily adjust a garment's length and width; it requires almost no seaming as well.

Knitting From the Top Down

MATERIALS

Provence by Classic Elite Yarns, 3½oz/100g hanks, each approx 205yd/187m (mercerized Egyptian cotton)

- 5 (6, 7, 8, 8, 9) hanks in #2633 sun-drenched yellow (MC)
- 2 (2, 3, 3, 4, 4) skeins in #2601 bleach (CC)
- One size 6 (4mm) circular needle, 32"/80cm length OR SIZE TO OBTAIN GAUGE
- One size 6 (4mm) circular needle, 16"/40cm length
- 4 stitch markers
- Scrap yarn or stitch holders

●●○○

Designed by Cathy Carron
Photographs by Paul Amato
Still-life photographs by Marcus Tullis

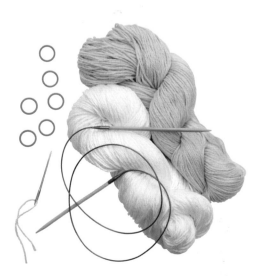

Sized for Small, Medium, Large, 1X, 2X and 3X. (Shown in size Small.)

MEASUREMENTS

- **Bust** 36 (40, 43¼, 48, 52, 56)"/91.5 (101.5, 110, 122, 132, 142)cm
- **Length** 24 (24¾, 26, 26¾, 28, 28½)"/61 (63, 66, 68, 71, 72.5)cm
- **Upper arm** 12½ (14, 15, 16, 17, 18)"/32 (35.5, 38, 40.5, 43, 45.5)cm

GAUGES

- 22 sts and 28 rows to 4"/10cm over St st using size 6 (4mm) needle.
- 21 sts and 28 rows to 4"/10cm over seed st using size 6 (4mm) needle.

TAKE TIME TO CHECK YOUR GAUGES.

NOTES

1) When changing colors, twist yarns on WS to prevent holes in work.
2) Use a separate bobbin for each color section. Do not carry yarn across back of work.
3) Sweater is worked in one piece from the neck down.

SEED STITCH

Row 1 *K1, p1; rep from * to end.
Row 2 K the purl sts and p the knit sts.
Rep row 2 for seed st.

BODY

With longer circular needle and CC, cast on 78 (82, 90, 94, 96, 106) sts for collar edge. Work in seed st for 13 rows.
Next row (WS) Working in seed st, work first 8 sts, inc 10 sts evenly to last 8 sts, work last 8 sts—88 (92, 100, 104, 106, 116) sts.

YOKE

Row 1 (RS) With CC, work in seed st for 8 sts, attach MC and working in St st, k10 (12, 13, 16, 17, 20) sts, place marker (pm), k7 (6, 7, 4, 2, 2) sleeve sts, pm, k38 (40, 44, 48, 52, 56) back sts, pm, k7 (6, 7, 4, 2, 2) sleeve sts, pm, k10 (12, 13, 16, 17, 20) sts, attach second ball of CC and k last 8 sts in seed st.
Row 2 (WS) With CC, work 8 sts in seed st, with MC and slipping markers, purl to last 8 sts, with CC, work last 8 sts in seed st.
Row 3 (inc row) With CC, work 8 sts in seed st, with MC, *k to 1 st before marker, k into front and back of next st (kfb), slip marker (sl m), kfb; rep from * 3 times more, knit to last 8 sts, with CC, work last 8 sts in seed st.
Rep inc row every other row 28 (29, 32, 35, 34, 36) times more, then every row 0 (3, 3, 4, 9, 10) times, working WS inc rows as foll:
Inc row 2 (WS) With CC, work 8 sts in seed st, with MC, *p to 1 st before marker, p into front and back of next st (pfb), slip marker (sl m), pfb; rep from * 3 times more, purl to last 8 sts, with CC, work last 8 sts in seed st.

A-Line Coat cont.

then at same edge every 5"/12.5cm twice more—18 (20, 22, 24, 26, 28) sts. Work even until piece measures 18"/45.5cm from beg, end with a WS row.

Shape armhole

Bind off 2 (2, 2, 3, 3, 3) sts at beg of next row. Work next row even. **Next (dec) row (RS)** K1, k2tog, work to end. **Next row** P1, work to end. Rep last 2 rows 1 (1, 1, 1, 2, 2) times more—14 (16, 18, 19, 20, 22) sts. Work even until armhole measures 5 (5½, 6, 6½, 7, 7½)"/12.5 (14, 15, 16.5, 18, 19)cm, end with a WS row.

Shape neck

Next row (RS) Work across first 9 (10, 12, 12, 13, 14) sts, place last 5 (6, 6, 7, 7, 8) sts on holder for left front neck. **Next row (WS)** P1, work to end. **Next (dec) row (RS)** Work to last 3 sts, ssk, k1. **Next row** P1, work to end. Rep last 2 rows once more—7 (8, 10, 10, 11, 12) sts. AT THE SAME TIME, when armhole measures 6 (6½, 7, 7½, 8, 8½)"/15 (16.5, 17.5, 19, 20.5, 21.5)cm, end with a WS row. Cont in k1, p1 rib, until piece measures same length as back to shoulder, end with a WS row. Place sts on holder for left shoulder.

RIGHT FRONT

Work as for left front, reversing all shaping by working A-line decs at end of RS rows, armhole shaping at beg of WS rows, and neck shaping at beg of RS rows.

SLEEVES

With larger needle, loosely cast on 29 (31, 33, 35, 37, 39) sts. Work back and forth in double seed st I for 7"/17.5cm, end with a WS row. Dec 1 st each side on next row, then every 8th row once more—25 (27, 29, 31, 33, 35) sts. Cont in k1, p1 rib for 1½"/4cm, end with a WS row.

Next (dec) row (RS) Cont in established rib for 11 (12, 13, 14, 15, 16) sts, p3tog (k3tog, p3tog, k3tog, p3tog, k3tog), cont in rib to end of row—23 (25, 27, 29, 31, 33) sts. Cont in k1, p1 rib as established for 3 rows. Inc 1 st each side on next row, then every 4th row once more—27 (29, 31, 33, 35, 37) sts. Work even until piece measures 18"/45.5cm from beg, end with a WS row.

Shape cap

Bind off 2 (2, 2, 3, 3, 3) sts at beg of next 2 rows. **Next (dec) row (RS)** K1, k2tog, work to last 3 sts, ssk, k1. **Next row** P1, work to last st, p1. Rep last 2 rows 3 (3, 3, 4, 4, 4) times more. Bind off 2 sts at beg of next 4 rows. Bind off rem 7 (9, 11, 9, 11, 13) sts.

FINISHING

Block pieces to measurements. Join left shoulder using three-needle bind-off as foll: Place sts from back left shoulder and front left shoulder onto needles. With RS facing, hold pieces on two parallel needles and so needles point to the right. Insert tip of 3rd needle knitwise into first st of each needle, and wrap yarn around needle as if to knit. Knit these 2 sts tog, then sl them off needles. *Knit next 2 sts tog in the same manner, then sl first st on 3rd needle over 2nd st and off needle; rep from * until all sts have been bound off. Rep for right shoulder.

Collar

With circular needle, cast on 5 sts, k 5 (6, 6, 7, 7, 8) sts from right front neck holder, pick up and k 8 sts along right neck edge, k 11 (11, 11, 13, 13, 13) sts from back neck holder, pick up and k 8 sts along left neck edge, k 5 (6, 6, 7, 7, 8) sts from left front neck holder—42 (44, 44, 48, 48, 50) sts. Do not join. Working back and forth, work row 1 of double seed st II. **Next (inc) row (RS)** K in front and back of next st, work row 2 of double seed st II to end—43 (45, 45, 49, 49, 51) sts. Work row 3 of double seed st II. **Next (buttonhole) row (RS)** Working row 4 of double seed st II, work first 2 sts, yo, k2tog, work to end. Work row 1 of double seed st II. **Next (dec) row (RS)** Sl 1, k1, psso, working row 2 of double seed st II, work to end—42 (44, 44, 48, 48, 50) sts. Work row 3 of double seed st II. Bind off in double seed st II.

Buttonband

With RS facing and smaller circular needle, pick up and k 54 (55, 56, 57, 58, 59) evenly spaced along entire left front edge, including side edge of collar. Do not join. Working back and forth, k next 2 rows. Bind off all sts loosely knitwise.

Buttonhole band

With RS facing and circular needle, pick up and k 48 (49, 50, 51, 52, 53) sts evenly spaced along right front edge ending below beg of collar. Do not join. Working back and forth, k next row. **Next (buttonhole) row (RS)** K 30 (31, 32, 33, 34, 35) sts, [yo, k2tog, k5] twice, yo, k2tog, k2. Bind off all sts loosely knitwise. Set in sleeves. Sew side and sleeve seams.

Buttons (make 4)

Make a slipknot leaving an 8"/20.5cm tail, then place loop on hook. Working fairly tightly, sc over cabone ring until ring is completely covered. Do not join. Cut yarn leaving a 8"/20.5cm tail, then thread this tail in tapestry needle. Sew running sts around outer edge, going under and over sc. Push outer edge over to WS and toward center of ring, then pull on tail to gather in edge and close opening at center. Fasten off tail securely on WS. Sew on buttons using rem 8"/20.5cm tails. On RS, sew bottom half of snap to top corner of left front collar. On WS, sew top half of snap to right front collar to correspond to bottom half. ✪

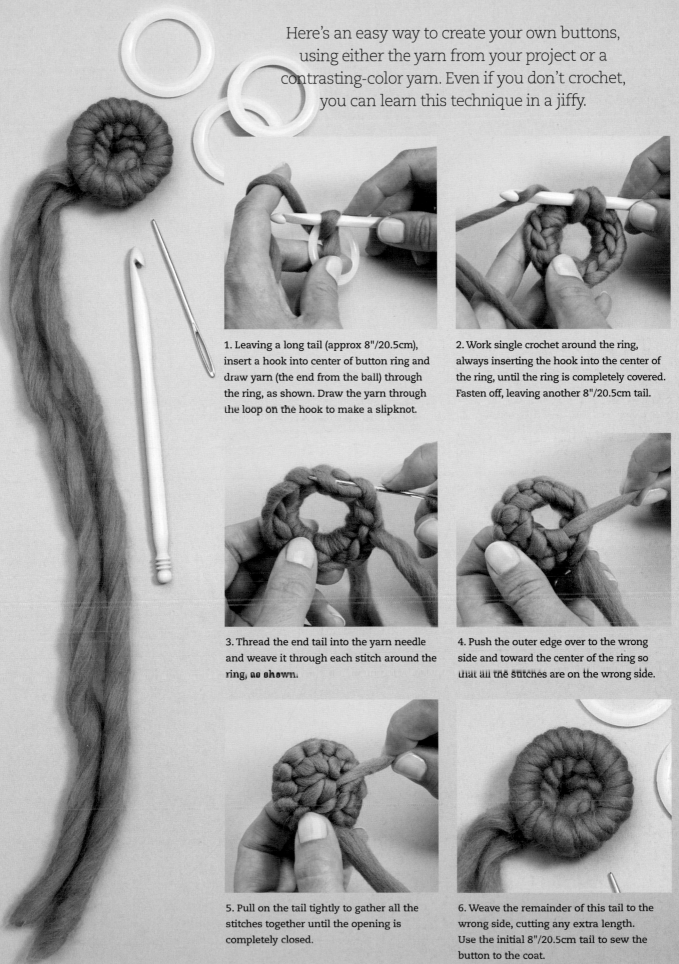

Here's an easy way to create your own buttons, using either the yarn from your project or a contrasting-color yarn. Even if you don't crochet, you can learn this technique in a jiffy.

1. Leaving a long tail (approx 8"/20.5cm), insert a hook into center of button ring and draw yarn (the end from the ball) through the ring, as shown. Draw the yarn through the loop on the hook to make a slipknot.

2. Work single crochet around the ring, always inserting the hook into the center of the ring, until the ring is completely covered. Fasten off, leaving another 8"/20.5cm tail.

3. Thread the end tail into the yarn needle and weave it through each stitch around the ring, as shown.

4. Push the outer edge over to the wrong side and toward the center of the ring so that all the stitches are on the wrong side.

5. Pull on the tail tightly to gather all the stitches together until the opening is completely closed.

6. Weave the remainder of this tail to the wrong side, cutting any extra length. Use the initial 8"/20.5cm tail to sew the button to the coat.

EASY TOPS

Having trouble making your shoulder seaming even? We show you two different seaming methods to ensure a perfect finished edge.

Finishing Touches

MATERIALS for turtleneck shell
Andean Alpaca Regal by Reynolds/JCA, Inc., 110yds/100g (alpaca/wool)
- 5(6, 6, 7, 8, 9, 10) hanks in #815 brick
- One pair each sizes 7 and 9 (4.5 and 5.5mm) knitting needles OR SIZE TO OBTAIN GAUGE
- Size 7 (4.5mm) circular needle, 16"/ 40cm length

●●○○

MATERIALS for cardigan
Andean Alpaca Regal by Reynolds/JCA, Inc., 110yds/100g (alpaca/wool)
- 12 (14, 16, 18, 19, 21, 23) hanks in #815 brick
- One pair each sizes 7 and 9 (4.5 and 5.5mm) knitting needles OR SIZE TO OBTAIN GAUGE
- Size 7 (4.5mm) circular needle, 16"/ 40cm length

●●●○

Photograph by Jack Deutsch
Still-life photographs by Marcus Tullis

TURTLENECK SHELL
Sized for X-Small, Small, Medium, Large, 1X, 2X, 3X. Shown in size Small.

MEASUREMENTS
- **Bust** 31 (35, 39, 44, 48, 52, 56)"/78.5 (89, 99, 111.5, 122, 132, 142)cm
- **Length** 19½ (20½, 21, 21½, 23, 23½, 24)"/49.5 (51.5, 53, 54.5, 58.5, 59.5, 61)cm

GAUGE
16 sts and 22 rows to 4"/10cm over St st using size 9 (5.5mm) needles. TAKE TIME TO CHECK YOUR GAUGE.

K2, P2 RIB (multiple of 4 sts plus 2)
Row 1 (RS) K2, *p2, k2; rep from * to end.
Row 2 P2, *k2, p2; rep from * to end. Rep rows 1 and 2 for k2, p2 rib.

K3, P3 RIB (multiple of 6 sts plus 3)
Row 1 (RS) K3, *p3, k3; rep from * to end.
Row 2 P3, *k3, p3; rep from * to end. Rep rows 1 and 2 for k3, p3 rib.

BACK
With smaller needles, cast on 63 (75, 81, 93, 99, 105, 117) sts. Work in k3, p3 rib for 2¾"/7cm, dec 1 (5, 3, 5, 3, 1, 5) sts evenly across last WS row— 62 (70, 78, 88, 96, 104, 112) sts. Change to larger needles and work in St st until piece measures 13, (13½, 13½, 13½, 14, 14, 14)"/33 (34, 34, 34, 35.5, 35.5, 35.5)cm from beg.

Shape armhole
Bind off 3 (3, 4, 5, 5, 6, 7) sts at beg of next 2 rows, 2 (3, 3, 3, 4, 4, 5) sts at beg of next 2 rows, 2 (2, 2, 3, 4, 4, 4) sts at beg of next 2 rows.
Dec row (RS) K3, k2tog, k to last 5 sts, ssk, k3. Work 1 row even. Rep last 2 rows 0 (2, 3, 5, 5, 7, 8) times more—46 (48, 52, 54, 58, 60, 62) sts. Work even until armhole measures 6½ (7, 7½, 8, 9, 9½, 10)"/16.5 (17.5, 19, 20.5, 23, 24, 25.5)cm. Bind off all sts, OR, if using 3-needle bind-off, place first and last 7 (8, 10, 10, 12, 13, 13) sts each side on a holder and bind off center 32 (32, 32, 34, 34, 34, 36) sts for neck.

FRONT
Work as for back until armhole measures 4½ (5, 5½, 6, 7, 7½, 8)"/11.5 (12.5, 14, 15, 18, 19, 20.5)cm.

Shape neck
Next row (RS) Work 17 (18, 20, 20, 22, 23, 23) sts, join 2nd ball of yarn and bind off center 12 (12, 12, 14, 14, 14, 16) sts, work to end. Working both sides at once, bind off from each neck edge 4 sts twice.
Dec row (RS) Work to last 5 sts of first half, ssk, k3; on 2nd half, k3, k2tog, k to end. Work 1 row even. Rep dec row. Work even of rem 7 (8, 10, 10, 12, 13, 13) sts each side until same length as back. Bind off (or place sts on a holder for 3-needle bind-off), for shoulders.

Diagram measurements
1¾ (2, 2½, 2½, 3, 3¼, 3¼)"
8 (8, 8, 8½, 8½, 8½, 9)"
FRONT & BACK
19½ (20½, 21, 21½, 23, 23½, 24)"
6½ (7, 7½, 8, 9, 9½, 10)"
10¼ (10¾, 10¾, 11¼, 11¼, 11¼)"
2¾"
15½ (17½, 19½, 22, 24, 26, 28)"

HOME

Don't touch that thermostat! Heat up your rooms with woolly décor in an array of eye-catching stitches.

Winter Pleasures

BASKETWEAVE PILLOW

MATERIALS

Montana by Tahki Yarns/Tahki•Stacy Charles, Inc., 3½oz/100g each approx 130yd/120m (100% unprocessed pure new wool)
- **3 hanks in #2 bark**

DOUBLE SEED STITCH PILLOW

MATERIALS

Montana by Tahki Yarns/Tahki•Stacy Charles, Inc., 3½oz/100g each approx 130yd/120m (100% unprocessed pure new wool)
- **3 hanks in #7 mint**

DIAGONAL RIB PILLOW

MATERIALS

Montana by Tahki Yarns/Tahki•Stacy Charles, Inc., 3½oz/100g each approx 130yd/120m (100% unprocessed pure new wool)
- **3 hanks in #1 natural**

BAMBOO STITCH PILLOW

MATERIALS

Montana by Tahki Yarns/Tahki•Stacy Charles, Inc., 3½oz/100g each approx 130yd/120m (100% unprocessed pure new wool)
- **3 hanks in #3 stone grey**

For each pillow:
- **One pair size 11 (7mm) knitting needles OR SIZE TO OBTAIN GAUGE**
- **Three 2"(50mm) buttons; one 16"/40.5 x 40.5cm pillow form and tapestry needle**

●●○○

Designed by Tanis Gray
Photographs by Paul Amato

BASKETWEAVE PILLOW

MEASUREMENTS

Approximately 16 x 16"/40.5 x 40.5cm

GAUGE

10 sts and 15 rows to 4"/10cm over basketweave pat using size 11 (7mm) needles.

BASKETWEAVE PATTERN (multiple of 6)
Rows 1 and 3 (RS) *P3, k3; rep from * to end.
Row 2 and all WS rows K the knit sts and p the purl sts.
Rows 5 and 7 *K3, p3; rep from * to end.
Row 8 Rep row 2. Rep rows 1–8 for basketweave pat.

PILLOW BACK

Cast on 41 sts. K1, work row 1 of basketweave pat to last 4 sts, end p3, k1. Cont to work in pat as established for 16"/40.5cm, knitting the first and last sts of each row for selvage st. Bind off in pat.

RIGHT FRONT

Cast on 26 sts. Knitting first and last st of each row for selvage st, work in basketweave pat until piece measures 16"/40.5cm from beg. Bind off in pat.

LEFT FRONT

Cast on 20 sts. Work same as for right front.

Buttonhole band

With the RS of the left front facing you, pick up and knit 34 sts through the bumps of the selvage sts along the right edge. Work 2 rows in k1, p1 rib.
Next (buttonhole) row (WS) Work 7 sts in rib as established, bind off next 2 sts, *work in rib until there are 7 sts on RH needle, bind off next 2 sts; rep from * once more, work in rib to end of row.
Next row Work in k1, p1 rib as established, casting on 2 sts over the bound-off sts in the previous row. Cont in rib for 2 more rows, Bind off in pat.

FINISHING

With RS facing you, sew the RH edge of the right front to the LH edge of the back piece. Sew the LH edge of the left front to the RH edge of the back piece. With the WS tog, sew the top and bottom of the right front to the top and bottom of the back. Sew the top and bottom of the left front to the top and bottom of the back, overlapping the right front with the buttonhole band. Attach buttons to right front opposite buttonholes. ✪

DOUBLE SEED STITCH PILLOW

MEASUREMENTS

Approximately 16 x 16"/40.5 x 40.5cm

**NATURAL PILLOW:
DIAGONAL STITCH**
Stripes of stockinette and reverse stockinette are knit on the diagonal and highlighted by traveling bands of double seed stitch.

**MINT PILLOW:
DOUBLE SEED STITCH**
This textured stitch alternates K1, P1 every two rows.

**STONE GRAY PILLOW:
BAMBOO STITCH**
Columns of knit stitch separated by purl strips resemble bamboo shoots once they're crossed by staggered rows of purls.

**BARK PILLOW:
BASKETWEAVE STITCH**
This version sports a classic basketweave checkerboard of small knit/purl blocks.

HOME

Winter Pleasures cont.

GAUGE

10 sts and 16 rows to 4"/10cm over double seed st pat.
TAKE TIME TO CHECK YOUR GAUGE.

DOUBLE SEED STITCH (even number of sts)

Row 1 (RS) *K1, p1; rep from * to end.
Row 2 K the knit sts and p the purl sts.
Row 3 *P1, k1; rep from * to end.
Row 4 K the knit sts and p the purl sts.
Rep rows 1–4 for double seed stitch.

PILLOW BACK

Cast on 40 sts. K1, work row 1 of double seed st pat to last st, k1. Cont to work in pat as established for 16"/40.5cm, knitting the first and last sts of each row for selvage st. Bind off in pat.

RIGHT FRONT

Cast on 26 sts and work as for back.

LEFT FRONT

Cast on 20 sts and work as for back.

FINISHING

Work buttonhole band and finish as for basketweave pillow. ✪

DIAGONAL RIB PILLOW

MEASUREMENTS

Approximately 16 x 16"/40.5 x 40.5cm

GAUGE

10 sts and 17 rows to 4"/10cm over diagonal stripe pattern.

PILLOW BACK

Cast on 38 sts. K1, work row 1 of diagonal rib chart to last st, k1. Cont to work in pat as established for 16"/40.5cm, knitting the first and last sts of each row for selvage st. Bind off in pat.

RIGHT FRONT

Cast on 20 sts and work same as for back.

LEFT FRONT

Cast on 20 sts and work same as for back.

FINISHING

Work buttonhole band and finish as for basketweave pillow. ✪

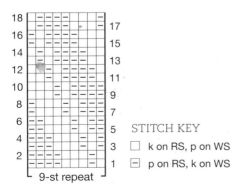

STITCH KEY
☐ k on RS, p on WS
⊟ p on RS, k on WS

9-st repeat

BAMBOO STITCH PILLOW

MEASUREMENTS

Approximately 16 x 16"/40.5 x 40.5cm

GAUGE

10 sts and 16 rows to 4"/10cm over double seed st pat.
TAKE TIME TO CHECK YOUR GAUGE.

BAMBOO STITCH (multiple of 12 plus 6)

Rows 1, 3, 7, and 9 (RS) *P2, k4; rep from * to end.
Rows 2, 4, 8, and 10 *P4, k2; rep from * to end.
Row 5 *P8, k4; rep from *, end p6.
Row 6 K6, *p4, k8; rep from * to end.
Row 11 P2, *k4, p8; rep from * end k4.
Row 12 *P4. k8; rep from *, end p4, k2.
Rep rows 1–12 for bamboo stitch.

PILLOW BACK

Cast on 44 sts. K1, work row 1 of bamboo st pat to last st, k1. Cont to work in pat as established for 16"/40.5cm, knitting the first and last sts of each row for selvage st. Bind off in pat.

RIGHT FRONT

Cast on 32 sts and work same as for back.

LEFT FRONT

Cast on 20 sts and work same as for back.

FINISHING

Work buttonhole band and finish as for basketweave pillow. ✪

pillow talk: tips for a perfect finish

1 BASKETWEAVE PILLOW

1) To sew cast-on edges together, insert needle under cast-on edge of one piece and into bump of purl stitch. Draw yarn through the fabric and tighten to close the seam.

2

2) Work into the two loops of the knit stitch on the edge of the other piece.

1 DOUBLE SEED STITCH PILLOW

1) To cast on stitches for the buttonhole, wrap yarn around your left thumb and place it on the needle.

2

2) On the following row, purl into the back loop of each cast-on stitch to make the edge more even.

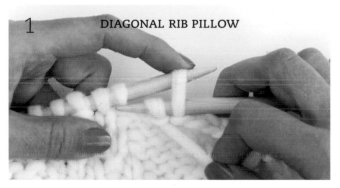

1 DIAGONAL RIB PILLOW

1) After working a purl stitch, insert LH needle from behind into the 2nd st on the RH needle and pass it over the purl st.

2

2) After working a knit stitch, insert LH needle from the front and into 2nd st on RH needle and pass it over the knit st.

1 BAMBOO STITCH PILLOW

1) To seam along the garter-stitch edge, insert the needle into the bump of the stitch, alternating from one side to the other.

2

2) To pick up stitches along the garter-stitch edge, insert needle into bump as before, wrap yarn around needle and pull through onto needle.

With canvases this grand—supersized plaid, piped-up stripes—you can go for the bold when it comes to color.

Colorblocked Afghan

MATERIALS

Wool-Ease by Lion Brand Yarn Co., 3oz/85g skeins, each approx 197yd/180m (acrylic/wool)
- 8 skeins in #114 denim (A)
- 6 skeins in #122 sienna (B)
- 1 skein each in #172 lemongrass (C) and #173 sage (D)
- One pair size 8 (5mm) knitting needles OR SIZE TO OBTAIN GAUGE

COLORS USED ON THIS PAGE:

a) #151 grey heather; b) #153 black; c) #196 zinnia; d) #147 purple; e) #129 cocoa; f) #174 avocado; g) #188 paprika; h) #195 azalea pink; i) #177 loden; j) #99 fisherman; k) #111 navy; l) #138 cranberry

●○○○

A *Knit Simple* original design
Photographs by Paul Amato
Still-lifes by Marcus Tullis and David Lazarus

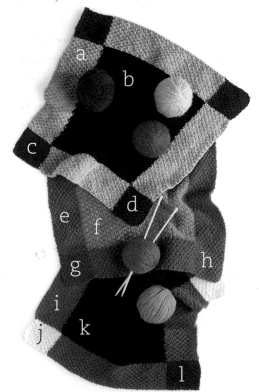

MEASUREMENTS

Approx 48" x 63"/122cm x 160cm

GAUGE

18 sts and 30 rows to 4"/10cm over moss st or double seed st using size 8 (5mm) needles.
TAKE TIME TO CHECK YOUR GAUGE.

MOSS STITCH

(over an even number of sts)
Row 1 (RS) *K1, p1; rep from * to end.
Row 2 Rep row 1.
Row 3 *P1, k1; rep from * to end.
Row 4 Rep row 3.
Rep rows 1–4 for moss st.

DOUBLE SEED STITCH

(over a multiple of 4 sts, plus 2)
Row 1 (RS) *K2, p2; rep from *, end k2.
Rows 2 and 3 *P2, k2; rep from *, end p2.
Row 4 Rep row 1.
Rep rows 1–4 for double seed st.

Notes

1) Color change should always occur on a WS row (that is, always k the knit st and p the purl sts with the new color).
2) All A sections are worked in double seed st; B, C and D sections are worked in moss st.

STRIPS 1 AND 5

With C, cast on 14 sts. Work in moss st for 21 rows, end with row 1 of pat. *Cut C, join B and cont in moss st for 90 rows (or 12"/30.5cm). Cut B, join D and cont in moss st for 22 rows. Cut D, join B and cont in moss st for 90 rows (or 12"/30.5cm). Cut B, join C and work in moss st for 22 rows; rep from * once more. Bind off with C.

STRIPS 3 AND 7

Work same as strips 1 and 5 but reverse colors C and D.

STRIPS 2, 4 AND 6

With B, cast on 54 sts. Work in moss st for 21 rows. *Cut B, join A and work next row on WS in moss st. Work in double seed st for 89 rows. Cut A, join B and work next row on WS in double seed st. Work in moss st for 21 rows; rep from * 3 times more. Bind off with B.

FINISHING

Sew strips tog foll placement diagram on following page. ✿

Afghans are the single most popular item to knit, and no wonder.
Easy stitching rarely delivers such impact.

Striped Afghan

MATERIALS

Washable Wool by Moda Dea/Coats & Clark,
3½oz/100g skeins, each approx 166yd/152m
(superwash wool)

- **10 skeins in #4441 lake blue (MC)**
- **5 skeins in #4461 maize (CC)**
- **One pair (or one long circular) size 8 (5mm) knitting needles OR SIZE TO OBTAIN GAUGE**

COLORS USED ON THIS PAGE:

a) #4423 aqua; b) #4453 tangerine;
c) #4435 taupe; d) #4465 coffee;
e) #4467 sage green; f) #4413 ivory

●○○○

A *Knit Simple* original design
Photographs by Paul Amato
Still-lifes by Marcus Tullis and David Lazarus

MEASUREMENTS

Approx 48" x 64"/122cm x 162.5cm

GAUGE

18 sts and 30 rows to 4"/10cm over seed st using size 8 (5mm) needles.
TAKE TIME TO CHECK YOUR GAUGE.

SEED STITCH

(over an odd number of sts)
Row 1 *K1, p1; rep from * to end.
Rep row 1 for seed st.

AFGHAN

With MC, cast on 217 sts. [With MC, work seed st for 5"/12.5cm.
With CC, work seed st for 5"/12.5cm] twice.
With MC, work seed st for 24"/61cm. [With CC, work seed st for
5"/12.5cm. With MC, work seed st for 5"/12.5cm] twice.
Bind off with MC.

FINISHING

With CC, work blanket st evenly around outside edge. ✿

colorblock afghan diagram (from previous page)

C	B	D	B	C	B	D	B	C	1
B	A	B	A	B	A	B	A	B	2
D	B	C	B	D	B	C	B	D	3
B	A	B	A	B	A	B	A	B	4
C	B	D	B	C	B	D	B	C	5
B	A	B	A	B	A	B	A	B	6
D	B	C	B	D	B	C	B	D	7

When it comes to patchwork, the whole is really the sum of its parts. And you're in control of those parts, for a completely custom outcome.

Mitered Square Afghan

MATERIALS

Encore Worsted by Plymouth Yarn, 3½oz/100g skeins, each approx 200yd/184m (acrylic/wool)

- **4 balls in #9408 rose (A) and #1607 magenta (B)**
- **2 balls in #999 burgundy (C)**
- **One pair size 8 (5mm) needles OR SIZE TO OBTAIN GAUGE**
- **Size H/8 (5mm) crochet hook**

Designed by Lisa Buccellato
Photographs by Rose Callahan
Still-life photographs by Marcus Tullis

MEASUREMENTS

Approximately 34 x 42.5"/86.5 x 108cm.

GAUGES

- 18 sts and 20 rows to 4"/10cm over garter st using size 8 (5mm) needles.
- Each square measures approx 4¼ x 4¼"/11 x 11cm.

TAKE TIME TO CHECK YOUR GAUGES

STITCH GLOSSARY

Sl 1 wyif Slip 1 st from LH needle to RH needle with yarn held in front.
S2KP (center double decrease) Slip 2 sts tog to RH needle, k next st, pass 2 sl sts over k1.

MITERED SQUARE

Cast on 21 sts, mark last st for center of square, cast on 20 sts—41 sts.
Row 1 (WS) Sl 1 st, k to marker, sl 1 wyif (center st), k to end.
Row 2 (RS) Sl 1 st, k to 1 st before marker, S2KP, k to end—39 sts. If necessary, remove marker to work S2KP, then replace marker in center st. Rep rows 1 and 2 until 3 sts rem, ready for a RS row.
Next row (RS) S2KP—1 st. Fasten off.

AFGHAN

Make 80 squares as foll: 32 each in A and B, 16 in C.

FINISHING

Arrange squares using photo and/or diagram as guide, sew together. With crochet hook, loosely work 1 row of sc around edge of afghan, skipping every other st. ○

Before we sewed up the squares, we laid a portion of them out in four

Mitered Square Afghan cont.

starburst diamonds

starburst diamonds

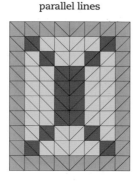

parallel lines

zigzag effect

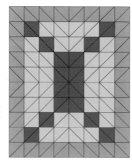

concentric lines

parallel lines

zigzag effect

different configurations (shown below). Orient the miters in a way that pleases your eye.

concentric lines

HOME

Even someone just starting out can master the basics of mosaic knitting to craft this stunning two-tone afghan.

Mosaic Afghan

MATERIALS

Decor by Patons, 3½oz/100g balls, each approx 210yd/189m (acrylic/wool)
- **7 balls each in #1622 dark blue (A) and #1620 light blue (B)**
- **One pair size 7 (4.5mm) needles OR SIZE TO OBTAIN GAUGE**

●●○○

Designed by Svetlana Avrakh
Photographs by Dan Howell

MEASUREMENTS

Approx 44½ x 59"/113cm x 150cm

GAUGE

20 sts and 36 rows to 4"/10cm over chart pat using size 7 (4.5mm) needles.
TAKE TIME TO CHECK YOUR GAUGE.

Notes

1) One row of chart represents two rows of knitting.
2) Work first row of chart (2 rows of knitting) with B, then cont to alternate 2 rows each A and B. See pages 126 and 127 for more details on mosaic knitting.

MOTIF (make 12)

With B, cast on 74 sts. K 1 row. Work in chart pat through row 160. Bind off in B.

FINISHING

Sew motifs in 3 strips, 4 in each strip. Sew strips together.
Top and bottom edging
With RS facing and A, pick up and k 153 sts along top of blanket. K 2 rows. Bind off knitwise on WS. Rep for botom of blanket.
Side edging
With RS facing and A, pick up and k 216 sts along side of blanket. K 2 rows. Bind off knitwise on WS. Rep for other side. ✪

colorways

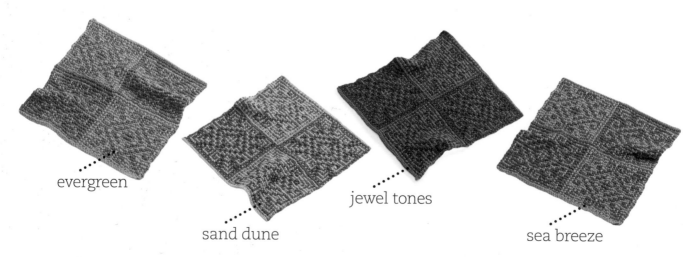

evergreen

sand dune

jewel tones

sea breeze

**159
& 160
with B**

**1
& 2
with A**

74 sts

Color Key

■ Dk blue (A)   □ Lt blue (B)

mosaic how-to

On this right-side row, knit the dark blue stitches and slip the light blue stitches with the yarn at the back.

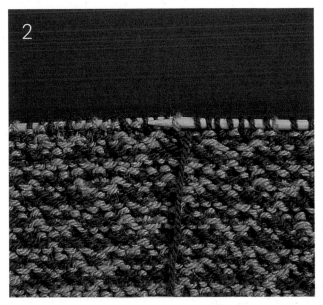

On the following wrong-side row, slip the light blue stitches with the yarn at the front of the work.

On this right-side row, knit the light blue stitches and slip the dark blue stitches with the yarn at the back.

On the following wrong-side row, be sure to bring the yarn to the back, between the needles, before knitting the next stitch.

Bursting with a spectrum of bright hues, this blanket
is composed of nine simple squares and a seven-round border.

Multicolored Granny-Square Afghan

MATERIALS

Cascade 220 by Cascade Yarns,
3½oz/100g hanks, each approx
220yd/201m (wool)

- **2 hanks in each in #8884 maroon (B), #7808 purple (C), #7827 yellow (D), #2403 chocolate (G) and #8907 turquoise (H)**
- **1 hank each in #7805 pink (A), #8914 green (E), #2414 russet (F) and #8505 off-white (I)**
- **Sizes K/10.5 (6.5mm) and L/11 (8mm) crochet hooks OR SIZE TO OBTAIN GAUGE**

●●○○

Photograph by Rose Callahan
Still-life photographs by Jack Deutsch

FINISHED MEASUREMENTS
54"/137cm square

GAUGE
1 square = 16"/40.5cm using larger hook.
TAKE TIME TO CHECK YOUR GAUGE.

SQUARE (make 9)
Note Work each square in the foll color sequence: A, B, C, D, E, F, G, H, A, B, C, D.
With larger hook and A, ch 5, sl st into first ch to form a ring. **Rnd 1 (RS)** Ch 3 (counts as first dc here and throughout), work 2 dc in ring, ch 2, [work 3 dc in ring, ch 2] 3 times, join with sl st to top of beginning ch, changing to B by drawing B through last 2 loops—12 dc. **Rnd 2** Ch 3, turn, (2 dc, ch 2, 3 dc) in first ch-2 sp, ch 1, [(3 dc, ch 2, 3 dc) in next ch-2 sp, ch 1] 3 times, join with sl st to top of beginning ch, changing to C—24 dc. **Rnd 3** Ch 3, turn, 2 dc in first ch-1 sp, ch 1, [(3 dc, ch 2, 3 dc) in next ch-2 sp, ch 1, 3 dc in next ch-1 sp, ch 1] 3 times, join with sl st to top of beginning ch, changing to D—36 dc. **Rnd 4** Ch 3, turn, 2 dc in first ch-1 sp, ch 1, *(3 dc, ch 2, 3 dc) in next ch-2 sp, ch 1, (3 dc in next ch-1 sp, ch 1) twice; rep from * around, join with sl st to top of beginning ch, changing to E—48 dc. **Rnd 5** Ch 3, turn, 2 dc in first ch-1 sp, ch 1, *(3 dc in next ch-1 sp, ch 1) across to next ch-2 sp, *(3 dc, ch 2, 3 dc) in next ch-2 sp, ch 1; rep from * around, join with sl st to top of beginning ch, changing to F—60 dc. **Rnds 6–12** Rep rnd 5, changing color every rnd according to the sequence above—144 dc. Fasten off.

FINISHING
With D, sew or crochet squares together in 3 rows of 3 squares each. Sew or crochet 3 rows together.

Border
Note Work border in the foll color sequence: I, E, F, G, H.
Hold afghan with RS facing. With larger hook and I, attach yarn with sl st to any ch-1 space. **Rnd 1** Ch 3, turn, 2 dc in same ch-1 sp, ch 1, *(work 3 dc in next ch-1 sp, ch 1) across to next corner ch-2 sp, (work 3 dc, ch 2, 3 dc) in corner ch-2 sp, ch 1; rep from * around, join with sl st to top of beginning ch, changing to E. **Rnds 2–5** Rep rnd 1, changing colors according to the Border sequence, turning after rnd 6 and changing to smaller hook. **Rnd 6** With H, sl st in each ch sp and dc around, join and fasten off. ✪

Lay two squares alongside each other
with the wrong sides facing.

Draw the yarn through all three loops on
the hook. We used a contrasting color.

This method of joining is quick and easy
and shows a neat and even seam.

A supersized set of squares makes a great introduction to this crochet technique—and will never fade into the background.

Giant Granny-Square Afghan

MATERIALS

Wool Semi Solids by Manos del Uruguay/Fairmount Fibers, Ltd., 3½oz/100g hanks, each approx 138yd/126m (wool)

- **2 skeins in #05 aqua (A)**
- **3 skeins each in #43 juniper (B) and #C powder (C)**
- **4 skeins in #Q calypso (D)**
- **5 skeins in #45 lapis (E)**
- **Size J/10 (6mm) crochet hook OR SIZE TO OBTAIN GAUGE**

●●○○

Photograph by Rose Callahan
Still-life photographs by Jack Deutsch

FINISHED MEASUREMENTS

61"/155cm square

GAUGE

Rnds 1–3 of blanket measures 4½"/11.5cm square using size J/10 (6mm) hook. TAKE TIME TO CHECK YOUR GAUGE.

BLANKET

With A, ch 4, join with sl st to first ch to form a ring.

Rnd 1 With A, ch 3 (counts as dc here and throughout), work 2 dc in ring, ch 2, [work 3 dc in ring, ch 2] 3 times, join with sl st to top of beginning ch—four 3-dc clusters.

Rnd 2 Sl st to first ch-2 sp, (work ch 3, 2 dc, ch 2, 3 dc) in first ch-2 sp, ch 1, *(work 3 dc, ch 2, 3 dc) in next ch-2 sp, ch 1; rep from * around, join with sl st to top of beginning ch—eight 3-dc clusters.

Rnd 3 Sl st to first ch-2 sp, (work ch 3, 2 dc, ch 2, 3 dc) in first ch-2 sp, ch 1, *(work 3 dc, ch 1) in next ch-1 sp, (work 3 dc, ch 2, 3 dc) in next ch-2 sp, ch 1; rep from * around, join with sl st to top of beginning ch—twelve 3-dc clusters.

Rnd 4 Sl st to first ch-2 sp, (work ch 3, 2 dc, ch 2, 3 dc) in first ch-2 sp, ch 1, *(work 3 dc, ch 1) in next two ch-1 sps, (work 3 dc, ch 2, 3 dc) in ch-2 sp, ch 1; rep from * around, join with sl st to top of beginning ch—sixteen 3-dc clusters.

Rnd 5 Sl st to first ch 2 sp, (work ch 3, 2 dc, ch 2, 3 dc) in first ch-2 sp, ch 1, *(work 3 dc, ch 1) in next three ch-1 sps, (work 3 dc, ch 2, 3 dc) in ch-2 sp, ch 1; rep from * around, join with sl st to top of beginning ch—twenty 3-dc clusters. Cont to work the square in the established pattern, working (3 dc, ch 2, 3 dc) in each corner ch-2 sp and working (3 dc, ch 1) in each ch-1 sp on sides of square. Join new colors of yarn in corner ch-2 sp and work in the following sequence: **Rnds 6–8** Color A. **Rnd 9** Color C. **Rnds 10–17** Color B. **Rnd 18** Color D. **Rnds 19–26** Color C. **Rnd 27** Color E. **Rnds 28–35** Color D. **Rnd 36** Color A. **Rnds 37–44** Color E. Fasten off.

Edging

Rnd 1 Attach B in any corner ch-2 sp. Ch 1, work 3 sc into each corner ch-2 sp and 1 sc into each dc and ch-1 sp, join with a sl st to first sc of rnd.

Rnd 2 *Skip next sc, 4 dc in next sc, skip next sc, sl st in next sc; rep from * around, join with sl st to first sc of previous rnd. Fasten off. ✪

Inserting the hook into the first chain while making the ring.

For joining, insert the hook into the two loops of the chain.

The chain 3 at the beginning of the round counts as one double crochet.

a

Hearth & Sole Stockings

Bring cheer to the chimney. Three stockings, knit from the same basic pattern, hang from I-cord loops with care.

Patterns A & B designed by Lori Steinberg
Pattern C designed by Faith Hale
Photographs by Paul Amato
How-to photographs by Marcus Tullis

b

C

Hearth and Sole: Stockings cont.

STOCKING A - POMPOM STOCKING
MATERIALS

Classic Wool by Patons, 3½oz/100g skeins, each approx 223yd/205m (wool)
- 1 skein in #204 old gold (A)
- 1 skein in #208 burgundy (B)
- 1 skein in #202 aran (C)
- One set (5) size 7 (4.5mm) double-pointed needles (dpns) OR SIZE TO OBTAIN GAUGE
- Stitch marker

●●○○

STOCKING B - BUTTON STOCKING
MATERIALS

Classic Wool by Patons, 3½oz/100g skeins, each approx 223yd/205m (wool)
- 1 skein in #240 leaf green (MC)

Beaver Fur by Fur Yarn by Paula Lishman, 1¾oz/50g hanks, each approx 25yd/23m (beaver fur)
- 1 hank in rose beige (CC)
- One set (5) size 7 (4.5mm) double-pointed needles (dpns) OR SIZE TO OBTAIN GAUGE
- One pair size 11 (8mm) needles
- Stitch marker
- Approx 40 white buttons in a mix of shapes and sizes
- Sewing needle and thread

●●○○

STOCKING C - CANDY CANE STOCKING
MATERIALS

Classic Wool by Patons, 3½oz/100g skeins, each approx 223yd/205m (wool)
- 1 skein each in #202 aran (A), #208 burgundy (B) and #240 leaf green (C)
- One set (5) size 7 (4.5mm) double-pointed needles (dpns) OR SIZE TO OBTAIN GAUGE
- Stitch marker

●●○○

STOCKING A - POMPOM STOCKING
MEASUREMENTS
- **Circumference 12"/30.5cm**
- **Length (cuff to heel) 16"/40.5cm**
- **Foot (heel to toe) 10"/25.5cm**

GAUGE
20 sts and 26 rnds to 4"/10cm over St st using size 7 (4.5mm) dpns.
TAKE TIME TO CHECK YOUR GAUGE.

STITCH GLOSSARY
K-fbf Inc 2 sts by knitting into front, then back, then front of next st.

BROKEN RIB
(over an even number of sts)
Rnd 1 Knit.
Rnd 2 *K1, p1; rep from * around.
Rep rnds 1 and 2 for broken rib.

STRIPE PATTERN
Rnds 1 and 2 With B, knit.
Rnds 3 and 4 With A, knit.
Rep rnds 1-4 for stripe pat.

CUFF
With A, cast on 60 sts, evenly distributed on 4 needles, pm and join, being careful not to twist. Work in broken rib until cuff measures 1"/2.5cm from beg. K 1 rnd.

LEG
(**NOTE** For smooth stripe transitions, see page 137.)
Beg stripe pat and work until piece measures 14"/35.5cm, end with a rnd 2.
Beg heel flap
Next rnd With C, k15 and turn. **Next row** Sl 1, p29, dropping marker for beg of rnds, and working all 30 heel sts onto one dpn. Leaving 30 sts for instep on hold, work back and forth on heel sts as foll:
Row 1 *Sl 1, k1; rep from * to end of row. **Row 2** Sl 1, p29. Rep rows 1 and 2 six times more, then row 1 once more.
Turn heel
Row 1 Sl 1, p16, p2tog, p1, turn. **Row 2** Sl 1, k5, SKP, k1, turn.
Row 3 Sl 1, p to 1 st before gap, p2tog, p1, turn. **Row 4** Sl 1, k to 1 st before gap, SKP, k1, turn. Rep rows 3 and 4 until all sts have been worked and 18 sts rem on heel needle.
Gusset
With free needle and C, pick up and knit 8 sts along edge of heel flap. With next needle and A, work in established

pat across 30 instep sts. Cont with A and established pat. With free needle, pick up and knit 8 sts along other edge of heel flap, k9 heel sts. PM for beg of rnds; with next needle, k9 heel sts and 8 gusset sts onto same needle, work to end of rnd, working instep sts back onto 2 separate needles if desired.

Next (dec) rnd Work to last 3 sts of first needle, k2tog, k1, work across instep sts, k1, SKP, k to end of rnd.

Work one rnd even in pat. Rep dec rnd once more—60 sts.

FOOT

Cont even until foot measures 9"/23cm from back of heel.

Toe shaping

Next rnd With C, *k8, k2tog; rep from * around. K one rnd. **Next rnd** *K7, k2tog; rep from * around. K one rnd. **Next rnd** *K6, k2tog; rep from * around. **Next rnd** *K5, k2tog; rep from * around. **Next rnd** K4, k2tog; rep from * around. Cont to dec in this manner every rnd until 6 sts rem. Cut yarn and thread through sts.

CUFF BAND

Make points

With C, make slipknot and place on needle, purl. *Next row (RS) K-fbf—3 sts. **Next row** Purl. **Next row** [Inc 1 in next st] twice, k1—5 sts. Purl one row. **Next row (RS)** Inc 1 in first st, k to last 2 sts, inc 1 in next st, k1. **Next row** Purl. Rep last 2 rows until there are 9 sts on needle, end with RS row. Cut yarn. Slide point to end of needle. Make slipknot and place on same needle, purl the slipknot. Rep from * until there are 6 points on needle. Do not cut yarn. **Next (joining) row** *P9, cast on 1 st; rep from * to end. Work in St st (k on RS, p on WS) until cuff band measures 1¼"/3cm from lowest point. Work 6 rows in garter st (k every row). Bind off. Block to shape points.

FINISHING

Pompoms

Make 3 pompoms using all 3 colors. Sew one pompom to every other point of cuff. Sew cuff band to cuff and seam tog at back.

I-cord loop

With MC, cast on 5 sts. *Knit one row. Without turning work, slide the sts back to beg of the row. Pull yarn tightly from the end of the row. Rep from * until I-cord measures 6"/15cm. Turn and work back and forth in garter st (k every row) for 1"/2.5cm. Bind off. Sew garter st tag to inside back of cuff. Form loop with I-cord and sew end to outside back of cuff. (See workshop on page 137.) ⊙

STOCKING B - BUTTON STOCKING
MEASUREMENTS
- **Circumference 12"/30.5cm**
- **Length (cuff to heel) 14"/35.5cm**
- **Foot (heel to toe) 10"/25.5cm**

GAUGE

20 sts and 26 rnds to 4"/10cm over St st using size 7 (4.5mm) dpns and MC.
TAKE TIME TO CHECK YOUR GAUGE.

CUFF

Cast on 60 sts, evenly distributed on 4 needles, pm and join, being careful not to twist. Work 6 rnds in garter st (k 1 rnd, p 1 rnd).
Change to St st (k every rnd) until cuff measures 2"/5cm from beg.
Work 4 more rnds in garter st

LEG

Change to St st and work until piece measures 12"/30.5cm.

Beg heel flap

Next rnd K15 and turn.

Next row Sl 1, p29, dropping marker for beg of rnds, and working all 30 heel sts onto one dpn.

Leaving 30 sts for instep on hold, work back and forth on heel sts as foll:

Row 1 *Sl 1, k1; rep from * to end of row.
Row 2 Sl 1, p29.
Rep rows 1 and 2 six times more, then row 1 once more.

Turn heel

Row 1 Sl 1, p16, p2tog, p1, turn. **Row 2** Sl 1, k5, SKP, k1, turn. **Row 3** Sl 1, p to 1 st before gap, p2tog, p1, turn. **Row 4** Sl 1, k to 1 st before gap, SKP, k1, turn. Rep rows 3 and 4 until all sts have been worked and 18 sts rem on heel needle.

Gusset

With free needle, pick up and knit 8 sts along edge of heel flap. With next needle, k across 30 instep sts. With free needle, pick up and knit 8 sts along other edge of heel flap, k9 heel sts. PM for beg of rnds; with next needle, k9 heel sts and 8 gusset sts onto same needle, k to end of rnd, working instep sts back onto 2 separate needles if desired.

Next (dec) rnd Work to last 3 sts of first needle, k2tog, k1, work across instep sts, k1, SKP, k to end of rnd.

Work one rnd even in pat. Rep dec rnd once more—60 sts.

FOOT

Cont even until foot measures 9"/23cm from back of heel.

Hearth and Sole: Stockings cont.

Toe shaping

Next rnd *K8, k2tog; rep from * around.
K one rnd.
Next rnd *K7, k2tog; rep from * around.
K one rnd.
Next rnd *K6, k2tog; rep from * around.
Next rnd *K5, k2tog; rep from * around.
Next rnd K4, k2tog; rep from * around.
Cont to dec in this manner every rnd until 6 sts rem.
Cut yarn and thread through sts.

FINISHING

Fur cuff

With size 11 needles and CC, cast on 4 sts. Work in garter st (k every row) until piece measures 12"/30.5cm or length to fit around cuff of stocking. Bind off.
Sew on between the garter st sections of stocking cuff.

I-cord loop

See Pattern C, below.

Embellishments

Sew on buttons as desired. ✪

STOCKING C - CANDY CANE STOCKING

MEASUREMENTS

- **Circumference 12"/30.5cm**
- **Length (cuff to heel) 12"/30.5cm**
- **Foot (heel to toe) 10"/25.5cm**

GAUGE

20 sts and 26 rnds to 4"/10cm over St st using size 7 (4.5mm) dpns.
TAKE TIME TO CHECK YOUR GAUGE.

GARTER RIB

(over a multiple of 4 sts)
Rnd 1 *K2, p2; rep from * around.
Rnd 2 Knit.
Rep rnds 1 and 2 for garter rib.

CANDY CANE STRIPE

Rnds 1 and 2 With A, knit.
Rnds 3–6 With B, knit.
Rep rnds 1–6 for candy cane stripe.

CUFF

With C, cast on 60 sts, evenly distributed on 4 needles, pm and join, being careful not to twist. Work in garter rib until cuff measures 2"/5cm from beg.

LEG

(**NOTE** For smooth stripe transitions, see page 137.)

Beg stripe pat and work until piece measures 10"/25.5cm, end with a rnd 2.

Beg heel flap

Next rnd With C, k15 and turn. **Next row** Sl 1, p29, dropping marker for beg of rnds, and working all 30 heel sts onto one dpn. Leaving 30 sts for instep on hold, work back and forth on heel sts as foll:
Row 1 *Sl 1, k1; rep from * to end of row.
Row 2 Sl 1, p29.
Rep rows 1 and 2 six times more, then row 1 once more.

Turn heel

Row 1 Sl 1, p16, p2tog, p1, turn. **Row 2** Sl 1, k5, SKP, k1, turn.**Row 3** Sl 1, p to 1 st before gap, p2tog, p1, turn.
Row 4 Sl 1, k to 1 st before gap, SKP, k1, turn. Rep rows 3 and 4 until all sts have been worked and 18 sts rem on heel needle.

Gusset

With free needle and C, pick up and knit 8 sts along edge of heel flap. With next needle and B, k across 30 instep sts. With free needle and B, pick up and knit 8 sts along other edge of heel flap, k9 heel sts. PM for beg of rnds. Cont with B and candy cane stripe pat; with next needle, k9 heel sts and 8 gusset sts onto same needle, work to end of rnd, working instep sts back onto 2 separate needles if desired.
Next (dec) rnd Work to last 3 sts of first needle, k2tog, k1, work across instep sts, k1, SKP, k to end of rnd.
Work one rnd even in pat.
Rep dec rnd once more—60 sts.

FOOT

Cont even in stripe pat until foot measures 9"/23cm from back of heel.

Toe shaping

Next rnd Change to C, *k8, k2tog; rep from * around. K one rnd. **Next rnd** *K7, k2tog; rep from * around. K one rnd. **Next rnd** *K6, k2tog; rep from * around. **Next rnd** *K5, k2tog; rep from * around. **Next rnd** K4, k2tog; rep from * around.
Cont to dec in this manner every rnd until 6 sts rem.
Cut yarn and thread through sts.

FINISHING

I-cord loop

With C, cast on 5 sts. *Knit one row. Without turning work, slide the sts back to beg of the row. Pull yarn tightly from the end of the row. Rep from * until I-cord measures 6"/15cm. Turn and work back and forth in garter st (k every row) for 1"/2.5cm. Bind off. Sew garter st tag to inside back of cuff. Form loop with I-cord and sew end to outside back of cuff. (See workshop on page 137.) ✪

Stripe It Right

For a smooth transition when working stripes in the round, first twist the new color around the old, as shown above.

Knit the first stitch of the 2nd round through both the next stitch and the stitch in the row below, as shown.

Triangular Finish

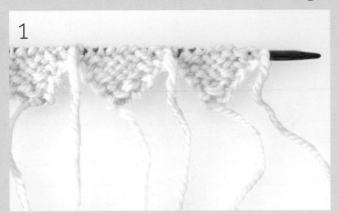

Six points are worked separately. To join, *p the sts of the next point, cast on 1 st; rep from * 5 times more.

To cast on, loop yarn around thumb. Insert RH needle from left to right, as shown. Remove thumb; pull stitch taut.

Easy I-Cord Tie

Once your I-cord with garter-st tag is finished, secure it firmly to the stocking with tapestry needle threaded with the end tail.

Sew tag to back of stocking cuff on WS, as shown, stitching all edges. Then, sew ½"/1.5cm of end of I-cord to cuff on RS.

Nicky Epstein's wreath spruces up the front door, welcoming revelers and carolers with nifty knitted berries, blooms and leaves.

Heart Felt

MATERIALS

Wool Clasica by Manos del Uruguay/ Fairmount Fibers, 3½oz/100g balls, each approx 138yd/126m (wool)
- **4 hanks in #101 jungle multi (A)**
- **3 hanks in #13 hunter (B)**
- **2 hanks in #66 poppy (C)**
- **1 hank each in #115 flame (D), #D spruce (E) and #40 goldenrod (F)**
- **One pair size 11 (8mm) needles OR SIZE TO OBTAIN GAUGE**
- **Beads from Bead Warehouse #17051 (105 beads)**
- **48" x 64"/122cm x 162.5cm piece of quilt batting (approx size), sewing thread, long needle**

●●○○

Designed by Nicky Epstein
Photograph by Jenny Acheson
Still-life photographs by Marcus Tullis

MEASUREMENTS
Approx 20" x 20"/51cm x 51cm

GAUGE
12 sts and 19 rows to 4"/10cm over St st using size 11 (8mm) needles. TAKE TIME TO CHECK YOUR GAUGE.

WREATH BASE
With A, cast on 45 sts. Work in St st for 70"/177.5cm. Bind off.

POINSETTIA
(make 5 complete poinsettias)
Petal (make 5 small petals, 5 large petals for each flower)
With C, cast on 3 sts. Work in St st, increasing 1 st each side every other row until there are 9 sts. Work even for small petal: 1½"/4cm, and for large petal; 2"/5cm, ending with a WS row.
Rows 1, 3 and 5 Ssk, k to last 2 sts, k2tog—3 sts rem after row 5.
Rows 2, 4 and 6 Purl.
Row 7 SK2P—1 st. Fasten off.

Poinsettia Berries (make 15 with F)
Cast on 1 st. K in front and back of same st until there are 5 sts. Work 4 rows in St st.
Next row P2tog, p1, p2tog, turn, k3tog. Fasten off. Using tail, weave through outer edge of berry, pull tightly to gather and shape berry. Tie tails together. Arrange 5 large petals in star shape. Arrange remaining 5 small petals on top of and offset form first 5 petals and sew in place. Attach berries to flower center so that rev St st faces outward.

POINSETTIA LEAVES (make 10)
With E make same as large poinsettia petal.

HOLLY LEAVES (make 29)
With B, cast on 7 sts.
Row 1 (RS) K3, yo, k1, yo, k3—9 sts.
Row 2 and all WS rows except rows 8, 14 and 20 Purl.
Rows 3, 9 and 15 K3, yo, k3, yo, k3—11 sts.
Rows 5, 11 and 17 K3, yo, k5, yo, k3—13 sts.
Rows 7 and 13 Bind off 3 sts, k2, yo, k1, yo, k 6—12 sts.
Rows 8 and 14 Bind off 3 sts, p 8—9 sts.
Row 15 K3, yo, k3, yo, k 3—11 sts.
Row 17 K3, yo, k5, yo, k 3—13 sts.
Row 19 Bind off 4 sts, [k1, yo] 2 times, k6—11 sts.

Heart Felt cont.

Row 20 Bind off 4 sts, p6—7 sts.
Row 21 Ssk, yo, SK2P, yo, k2tog—5 sts.
Row 23 Ssk, k1, k2tog—3 sts.
Row 25 SK2P—1 st. Fasten off.

HOLLY BERRIES (make 10)

With 2 strands D, work same as poinsettia centers.

FINISHING

Pin as you roll batting tightly and sew securely to hold in roll shape (should measure approx 8"/20.5cm around). Sew short ends of batting together to form circle. Sew knitted wreath together (cast-on edge to bind-off edge). Put batting wreath into knitted wreath and sew seam together and gather enough to shape a circle to fit loosely around poly batting. Batting should fit loosely into wreath.

FELTING

Felt all pieces (3 washes or until knit wreath fits poly batting wreath), as foll:
Fill washing machine to low water setting at a hot temperature. Add ½ cup of a gentle detergent. Add all pieces and a pair of jeans to provide abrasion and balanced agitation. Use 15–20 minute wash cycle, including cold rinse and spin. Check measurements of wreath. If it's still larger than finished measurements, repeat process with progressively shorter cycles, measuring every few minutes until measurement is achieved. Let air-dry.

ASSEMBLY

Following photo, with corresponding sewing thread sew pieces to wreath. Sew 7 beads to each center berry. ✪

Helpful Hints

- Prefelted fabric is always knit at a looser gauge than is normally recommended.
- Place the small embellishments in a lingerie bag or pillowcase before putting them in the washing machine.
- With two strands held together and a large crochet hook, make two 5"/12.5cm chains and felt. Sew chains into loops and attach to the back of the wreath, at the center top and center bottom. The second loop prevents the wreath from sagging when hung.
- Change colors and floral scheme for each season. Refer to *Nicky Epstein's Knitted Flowers* (Sixth&Spring Books) for ideas.

before felting/the inside story

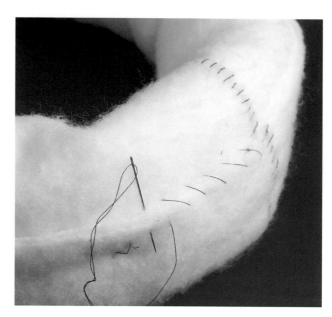

Roll quilter's batting into a tube approximately 60"/152.5cm long and 8"/20.5cm in diameter. Using a needle and thread, secure the tube with small basting stitches every 6"/15cm. Whipstitch beginning and end of tube together to form a circle. Next, whipstitch around circumference to secure batting.

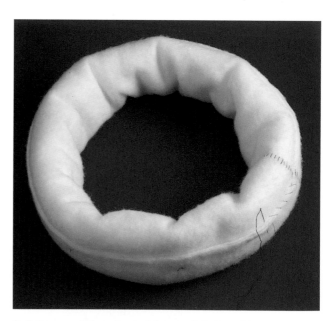

Knit the wreath base in stockinette stitch for 70"/178 cm. Wrap the knitted strip around the ring of batting and pin in place. Sew ends together. Whipstitch edges around the tube. Knit all the poinsettia pieces, holly leaves and berries.

petal felting

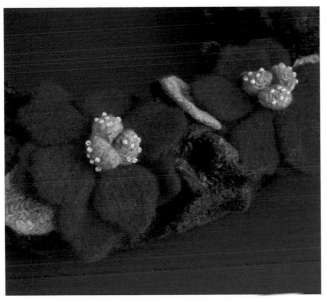

the final steps

To create the three-dimensional berries and flower centers, weave the tail through the outer edge of the berry; pull tightly to gather. The poinsettia petals are worked with two strands held together for extra texture. Felt all of the pieces by hand or in a washing machine. The knitted base should shrink around the batting; this may take up to three washings.

Following the photographs on these pages, attach the leaves, poinsettias and berries using a needle and thread in matching colors. Sew a cluster of beads to the center of each flower.

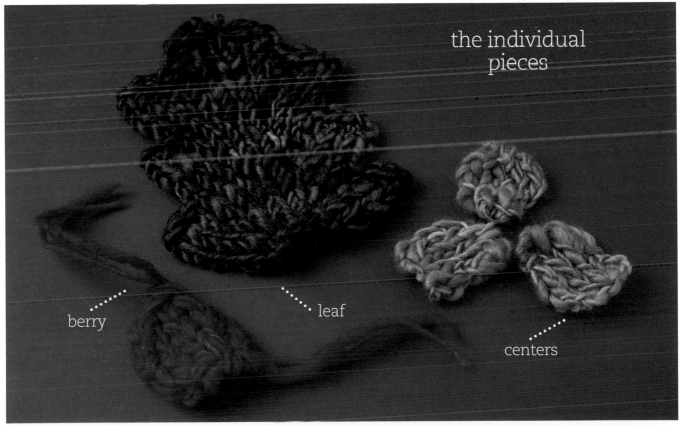

the individual pieces

berry

leaf

centers

Those important enough to make your gift list deserve good tidings in the form of hand-knit holiday cheer.

Embroidered Ornaments

MATERIALS

Soft Yarn by Red Heart/Coats & Clark, 5oz/140g, each approx 256yd/234m (acrylic)

- 1 ball each in #2515 turquoise, #4601 off white, #9522 leaf, #9537 fuchsia, #3720 lavender, #4412 grass green
- One set (5) size 7 (4.5mm) double-pointed needles (dpns) OR SIZE TO OBTAIN GAUGE
- Tapestry needle
- 8mm and 4mm sequins
- Silver 5-point star sequins
- Aleene's Original Tacky Glue
- Plastic grocery bags

Designed by Phoenix Bess
Photograph by Jenny Acheson

MEASUREMENTS

Circumference approx 12–13"/30.5–33cm

GAUGE

20 sts and 26 rnds to 4"/10cm over St st. TAKE TIME TO CHECK YOUR GAUGE.

ORNAMENT

With desired color, cast on 16 sts. Divide sts evenly over 4 needles, place marker and join for knitting in the round, taking care not to twist sts.

Rnd 1 and all odd rnds Knit.

Rnd 2 *K3, kfb (k in front and back of st); rep from * around—20 sts.

Rnd 4 *K4, kfb; rep from * around—24 sts. Cont in this way to inc 4 sts every other rnd, working 1 more st between inc every inc rnd, until there are 52 sts.

Rnd 20 *K11, k2tog; rep from * around—48 sts. **Rnd 22** *K10, k2tog; rep from * around—44 sts. Cont in this way to dec 4 sts every other rnd until 16 sts rem.

Cut yarn, leaving a 6"/15cm tail. Thread through rem sts and cinch tightly to close.

FINISHING

Stuff tightly with plastic bags through cast-on opening. With tapestry needle and MC, thread through cast-on sts and cinch tightly to close. Push yarn to inside of ornament and secure.

EMBROIDERY

Embroider designs on ornaments following diagrams (below) and in desired colors, using satin stitch for butterfly, berries and flower, straight stitch for stars and snowflakes, and cross stitch at ends of star. Glue (or sew) on sequins using photo for placement, or as desired. ✪

butterfly

holly berries

flower

light snowflake

star

snowflake

Mothers and grandmothers pass the torch, keeping the knitting flame alive.

What My Mother Taught Me

As told to Faith Hale

"I learned to love kitting from my grandmother. From the moment she got up in the morning until she went to bed at night, Grandma was always busy working with her hands, and it seemed to me that this was something that could occupy a lifetime. Today you can find me happily doing the very same things she did—constantly dreaming up something new and never, ever getting bored." **Mari Lynn Patrick,** *Knit Simple* **Contributing Patterns Editor**

"My mother taught me to knit but not to purl, so indirectly she encouraged me to learn on my own. She instilled in me a desire to seek out that knowledge independently. Little did I know then what a great example that would set for life. Thanks, Mom." **Lily Chin, Designer**

"I learned many important things from my mother [knitting legend Elizabeth Zimmermann]: You are in charge of your own knitting; there is no 'wrong' in knitting; knitting is a pleasure—don't take it too seriously." **Meg Swansen, Designer**

"My mother taught me to knit by using the verse 'Peek through the window, once around the back, go back through the window and off jumps Jack.' Every time I teach someone to knit, I share the same rhyme." **Tanis Gray, Designer**

"My advice, which I learned from my own daughter, is to be brave. Explore outside the rules, and don't ever be afraid to try something new or to make mistakes. You never know where they will lead you. After all, it's only knitting. You can always rip out." **Linda Medina, Designer**

"When my daughter Phoenix taught me to knit, I learned grudgingly, only so I could keep her company in her new endeavor. But my prejudice against the craft quickly turned to devotion as I discovered the glories of texture, color and design. Phoenix taught me that knitting is not only a genuine medium of artistic expression but the door to a womanly world of camaraderie and community." **Beth Bess, Bella Blue Collection**

"My grandma is my favorite person to knit for, as she uses, shows off and displays all of the items I have knit for her—even the ones that didn't turn out so well. For instance, every year she gets out the cotton potholders I made for her years ago, complete with beginner mistakes, and uses them on the buffet table at Christmas, right along with her best china and silver." **Amy Polcyn, Designer**

"The most important lesson my mother taught me is that patience and practice will always pay off. She encouraged me to persevere even when my knitting began with twenty stitches and ended with five." **Pat Harste, Designer**

"The greatest lesson my mom taught me is that if it's not right, rip it out and redo it, no matter what. Your knitting is worth it." **Jared Flood, Designer**

"My mother wasn't a knitter, but she was a fantastic seamstress. Her work was always perfection, every last thread snipped and crease pressed. She passed on to me a deep sense of pride in my own handmade creations. Being proud of what you do or make will take you far in life." **Susan B. Anderson, Designer**

yarn+life+fun

KnitSimple Magazine

Editor in Chief CARLA SCOTT
Creative Director JOE VIOR
Managing Editor LESLIE A. BARBER

Knitting Editor
ROSEMARY DRYSDALE
Yarn Editor
RENEE LORION
Patterns Editor
LORI STEINBERG
Technical Editor
LORETTA DACHMAN
Technical Coordinator
LISA BUCCELLATO
Associate Editor
FAITH HALE
Fashion Editor
SARAH LIEBOWITZ
Contributing Patterns Editor
MARI LYNN PATRICK
Contributing Editor
CHERYL KREMENTZ

sixth&spring books

President ART JOINNIDES
Vice President/Publisher TRISHA MALCOLM
Chairman JAY H. STEIN
Production Director DAVID JOINNIDES

Cover Design JOY MAKON
Cover Photography JACK DEUTSCH

copyright © 2011 by Sixth&Spring Books
All rights reserved.
Originally published as KnitSimple Knitting Workshops for Knit Simple magazine, in 2010.
No part of this book may be copied or reproduced by any means—graphic, electronic, or mechanical, including photocopying or recording, or information storage-and-retrieval systems, without written permission of the publisher.

The written instructions, photographs, designs, projects and patterns are intended for the personal noncommerical use of the retail purchaser and are under federal copyright laws; they are not to be reproduced in any form for commercial use. Permission is granted to photograph patterns solely for the personal use of the retail purchaser. Garments knit from patterns in this book are for personal use only and cannot be sold.

Library of Congress Control Number:
2011927551

ISBN 13: 978-1-936096-28-2
ISBN 10: 1-936096-28-5

Manufactured in China
1 3 5 7 10 8 6 4 2